A Deeper Walk

GOD. LIFE. PROGRESSIVE CULTURE.

A Deeper Walk

FAMILY CHRISTIAN STORES
www.FamilyChristian.com

Published by Family Christian Stores, 5300 Patterson Avenue SE, Grand Rapids, Michigan 49530.

ISBN 1593910142

1 2 3 4 5 6 7 8 9 10

Dear Valued Guest,

For more than seventy years, Family Christian Stores has had the privilege of impacting lives for Christ as a ministry-minded business. For this reason, we take extra care to offer one of the widest selections of Christian products designed to strengthen the hearts, minds and souls of believers and seekers from all ages and stages of life. This book you now hold in your hand is an extension of our mission. The *Hearts, Minds & Souls* series is an exclusive collection of books created to engage our guests in transforming and redemptive relationships with our Savior, Jesus Christ.

In addition to this book, the over ten thousand different products available in our stores and through FamilyChristian.com website provide a wealth of additional resources to address every need from a faith-filled, Christ-centered perspective. We have Bibles for everyone from young children just learning to read to seminary students serious about every nuance of Greek and Hebrew. We even have Bible accessories like covers, highlighters, tabs and more. We have books for men and women, singles and married couples, kids, tweens, teens and adults. We have music to minister to the hearts of every rhyme and rhythmical preference. From cards to tees, household items to framed art, pens to games, whatever your need, we promise you'll find something to enrich and enhance your lifestyle at Family Christian Stores.

We're also sensitive to your desire to be a good steward of the resources God has given you. That's why we offer a price matching promise, exclusive Perks program and great monthly deals on the latest most popular books and music.

Thank you for shopping Family Christian Stores and FamilyChristian.com. We appreciate your partnership in reaching families and communities with the gospel and grace of Jesus Christ. We ask that you pray for us as we seek to operate our company in a way that best fulfills the mission God has given us.

Answering the call to help strengthen
the hearts, minds & souls of our guests,

Dave Browne

Dave Browne
President/CEO
Family Christian Stores

CONTENTS

God of the Dark Places

Foreword By Dan Haseltine of Jars of Clay

» I sat in the chair anxious for what was about to take place. I tried not to think about the impending pain. I just stared at the wall adorned with the artistic statements born under the skin of those who came before me. As I took in all of the magnificent designs and intricate sketches, a feeling of inferiority came over me. My design was simple. It was just two Chinese characters. I watched the man in a chair next to me getting some touch-ups to the bikini-clad woman riding the rhino skeleton he had branded across his chest. I began rolling in my mind the host of different reactions I would get from family members, friends, and even strangers. I am not sure what kept me in the chair. Perhaps it was pride. If I had gotten up, I would have had to face the jibes of friends, and come to grips with the fact I was not man enough to go through with it. So, I sat. I waited for nearly thirty minutes. Long enough to really build up in my mind how painful it would be. I created a vision of a giant needle burrowing into my skin. I remembered the torture scene from the movie Braveheart. I pictured the tattoo artist standing over me dressed in a burlap robe, telling me if I did not surrender he would paint a giant turkey vulture across my chest. I thought about screaming "Freedom!"

I handed him the piece of paper upon which I had drawn my simple design of two Chinese characters symbolizing salt and light. I was expecting to be questioned about my choice of design. I knew people had gotten Chinese symbols before, but salt was somewhat unusual. Without a word he began creating the template. I scanned the wall of designs one more time, looked over my shoulder at the nearly finished rhino-skeleton-riding beach blonde, and realized the artists probably stopped inquiring about the designs they were inking a long time ago. He finished the template. We settled on a location just up from the watch line on the inside of my right arm. Highly visible. "Do you want other people to read it or do you want to read it?" I responded, "Other people should not have to read it." He did not quite understand what I meant. He just turned the image around and made the imprint on my arm.

He fired up the bludgeoning device and went to work. I was amazed at his skill, speed, and accuracy as he pushed the needle back and forth around the curvature of the design. He was truly an artist. I was also very relieved to know the pain would be over soon. But I suppose art has never been born without some form of pain attached to it.

To some, tattoo parlors represent the dregs of society, the epitome of our sinful nature along with the porn shops and strip clubs, bars, and psychic reading kiosks. These are places that drip poison into the hearts and minds of those struggling to live a life of pure thought and deed. They are entrees in the buffet of destructive temptations, places where some might conclude darkness has found a way to eclipse light. Many of us have come to believe these are unlikely places to find real beauty, or any redemptive power working.

Upon the walls of Sunset Strip Tattoo Parlor under the fluorescent lights there exists a parable of God's grace and mercy. It finds voice in every painful pierce of a needle and in every birth of an intricate design. It is unearthed in the testimony of skilled craftsmanship and in branded expressions inked across the skin of searching souls. Where there is beauty there is God. Where there is creation there is God. Where there is searching there is God. Where there is God there is passion, fire, and an overwhelming sense that He is good, but not safe. In these places God has made Himself known as One who cares little to restrict Himself in His approach to redemption by working only in ways we, His creation, would dub appropriate or possible. God's story has always been placed upon the backdrop of unlikely places. This is true whether we understand it, approve of it, and see it, like it or not.

Because of God's commitment to loving people in wild and unpredictable ways, we His people must carry with us an image of God that is wild with jealousy, undeniably reckless and methodically unpredictable in the approach to pursuing the lost watching world. Have we as image bearers laid claim to these very same characteristics? Have we come to know the God of parting seas, and burning bushes? Have we come to know the God of treacherous storms, and resurrections? He is good. He is not safe.

Within the structure of the modern church a stray belief has developed regarding effective ministry. It is a completely recognizable tattoo on the outer skin of the evangelical community. It presupposes that the qualifying attribute of effective evangelism is a squeaky clean image. It implies we are good witnesses for Christ only when we have our world in proper perspective, our spiritual life in order, and our suit dry cleaned and pressed. It is this doctrine that cuts at the Achilles heel of true faith. The Gospel has always been about one beggar showing another beggar where to find food. The Gospel of salvation only matters to those who are aware of their need of rescue. I would venture to say that the idea of such perfect imaging was created by people who have long forgotten they too are in constant need of rescue.

God has chosen liars and thieves, lepers, and whores to tell the story of his love. He uses the blind and the deaf, the homeless and the greedy, the selfish and the faithless. He has used evil kings and lowly shepherds. He has used simple-minded children and self-righteous priests. These are the imperfect conduits of God's love and mercy. The people of God's wild redemption tale are an equally unlikely cast. This was true to form in the story of Jonah.

A supply boat set sail from the port of Joppa to Tarshish carrying a few travelers and a small crew. The crewmembers were storing last-minute supplies while the last of the paying travelers climbed aboard. It was a calm morning and the sea was quiet this time of year. A bell rang the final call as a pale, slightly disheveled man ran down the dock and dropped a few coins out of his sweaty hand into the shipmates rusty bucket. He climbed down the plank as his eyes scanned the lively deck. Having noticed there was little activity down below, he climbed down the ladder and took a spot in a dimly lit corner away from the other travelers. Once they were at sea, He would rest. He had been running for a long time. His bones ached like winter, and his head was heavy with the kind of purpose only guilt could birth. He began to feel the gentle rocking of the vessel. His eyes grew heavy and he fell fast asleep. While he slept, a great wind came across the water and swirled the sea and sky into a violent storm. The crewmembers and travelers all began to pray to their gods to be delivered from this angry cloud. It was as if the waves had made a deal with the wind so that they would all be carried to crest upon the boat from any direction. With every futile prayer came more waves, and more wind. The boat was threatening to break apart, so they cried out again, "Who has caused such misfortune to come to us?" They cast lots and found blame in the one man fast asleep below deck. Jonah was awakened by his accusers and brought to the upper deck. "Who are you? What have you done?" they asked. "I am a Hebrew and I worship the Lord, the God of heaven, who made the sea and the land."

To understand the significance of this moment we must first be introduced to the person of Jonah. He was a minister of God who found himself so deep inside the moral law of religion that he could not make a way to love God's plan of grace and forgiveness. He hated the idea that perpetual sinners could receive God's ever-flowing gift of perpetual mercy.

The story of Jonah begins by stating: "The word of the Lord came to Jonah, 'Go to the great city of Nineveh and preach against it, because its wickedness has come up before Me.' But Jonah ran away from the Lord and headed for Tarshish. He went down to Joppa and found a ship heading for that port. After paying the fare, he went aboard and sailed for Tarshish to flee the Lord" (JONAH 1:1-3). Jonah hated the city of Nineveh. He hated the people of that great city with a deep-seated passion. He wanted to see them burn in hell. He did not want to preach to them because he knew that meant God would forgive them and show mercy to them. Jonah knew he would have to love these people. He would be the vessel sharing with them living water, salvation for their souls. Jonah wanted absolutely no part of that. So he ran.

A mentor of mine once spoke to me about leadership. He said you can tell a true leader by his reluctance to be in a position of leadership. Be wary of those too comfortable with being in such positions of power. True leaders know what is required of them. They understand that the model of leadership Jesus Christ set up for us was one of servitude. They know that leadership is far less about visible strength than it is about transparent weakness. To be a leader the will must be crushed. The resistance to die to our own purpose that continues to grow must be reckoned with on a continual basis. Jonah was an example of a man who knew what was required of him.

But God gave Jonah a gift. Just before Jonah is thrown into the sea and swallowed by a giant fish, God showed Jonah how far He would go to reach the lost. God opens Jonah's eyes to how wild and unpredictable His schemes can become. By using such blatant rebellion along with Jonah's own testimony about the God he served, He brought salvation to the wandering sailors caught in Jonah's storm.

For my tattoo, I chose Chinese symbols to remind me of the God I met among the people of the underground church in China—a magical, aggressive, merciful God who could bring such vivid joy in the midst of suffering and laughter in the presence of injustice and true freedom in the clutches of political slavery. Salt reminds me that through Christ I have the power and the great pleasure of seasoning life with passion. And light is the only thing people search for in the dark places of the world.

We, the Body of Christ, have all faced the stifling opinion of order. Age-old traditions have chipped away at us and we have come to believe something as wild as love could be contained in patterns and rituals. We have come to believe something as intoxicating and explosive as saving grace could be bound and gagged like a hostage to only our altar calls and rededication ceremonies.

The Church has lost its power to love because we have rendered the God of love powerless by covering the only truth that speaks to the depths of the heart and soul in a shroud of pious doctrine, false-righteousness, religious politics, and moral policing. We have gotten so exclusive in our insular Christian lifestyle we have given real people with real issues no alternative but to deem the Gospel irrelevant or inconsequential.

There is a sense of hopelessness about the modern church in America. A feeling that those who came before have set an irreversible perception in place by which the world will perpetuate its angry biases. If you share in this despair I pray that this book will encourage you. The Church is very much a main character in the story of salvation and redemption.

We are standing at a point in history. A line has been drawn in the sand. It is now the time to reclaim the real attributes of Christ. We have seen the great divide created in our culture between the Body of Christ and the watching world. It is our turn to build bridges and believe in a love that drives out fear, a love that seeks not to convert, not to fill church buildings, not to make people think like we do, but simply to love as far as God will reach. We need to give up the "us against them" mentality. Let us assume the posture of a beggar showing another beggar where to find food. We must attempt to fulfill real needs, and have faith God will call His own to Himself. For the labyrinth of the heart is severely complex, and the wounds run deep. God alone can bind up the broken hearted. We must simply seek to serve. Our honesty, transparency, and love are what drive us to true relevance in a cynical, jaded post-Christian culture.

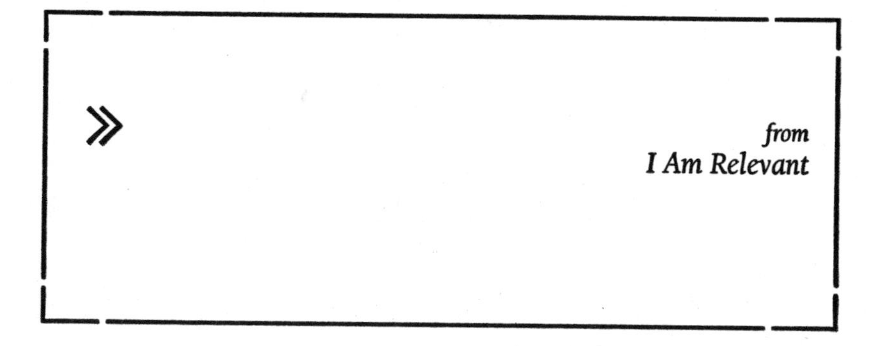

Dan Haseltine is the frontman of the multi-platinum and Grammy-winning band, Jars of Clay. Over the past few years, the band has also been recognized for their humanitarian efforts that extend globally.

Deeper Walk

By Winn Collier

We have lost what it means to live. Thus we have lost what it means to die.

In *Working the Angles*, Eugene Peterson laments the loss of the day "when pastoral work was defined as preparing people for a good death." There seems to be little demand for this type of pastoral vocation. It's a shame because eternity waits on the other side of the hearse.

We hear a haunting whisper in our hearts that life is more than a portfolio, a title, or a pristine spiritual image. It has become cliché to acknowledge our need for a slower pace, a more reflective encounter with the world and people around us. Yet seldom does this cliché translate to an *actual* slower pace. And the art of reflection, for most of us, is like Shakespeare: we all agree he's good, but *read* him? Few of us actually have.

For years, those who care about our spiritual life have warned us of the peril we are inviting. Like the lonely voice of Noah, these prophets have called us to stop, to look around us, and to look at ourselves. They are convinced if we would only look...we would be terrified by what we saw. And we would listen. But we refuse to stop, and we certainly refuse to look. And so, we ignore their warnings. And the dark rain clouds hover on the horizon.

Why is this our lot? Why do we press harder and move faster, knowing all along it is killing our souls? Despite being convinced there is a desperate need to pause, why do we only press harder on the pedal?

What are we running after?

Better yet, what are we running from?

I suspect we are running from ourselves. The biggest lie we have believed is not that we need to get more, achieve more, or be more, as hideous as those are. The biggest lie we have believed is that life depends on us. We have succumbed to the ancient deception, winding all the way back to a garden, a tree, and the greatest tragedy ever told.

"God isn't good. He's holding out on you. You're on your own."

The lie was believed, and the fruit was taken. And we have followed the elusive fruit ever since. So we can never pause long enough to look at the world we have created for ourselves because our heart knows that if life really depends on us, we are certainly doomed. And so we run.

What they needed in the garden is still all we need today: God. Yet in believing the delusion that life is found in everything other than God, we seal our fate. In the garden, life was never so good as the cool evening walks with the Creator. In modern life, those quiet connections with God offer the same balm, the same sense of wholeness.

After the great tragedy when God was refused and destruction unleashed, what our oldest father and mother desperately needed is again all we need today: mercy. Yet if we insist that life is all about us, we refuse mercy. We never see the need for it. It is simply a word, void of power, void of healing.

And at the end of our days, we have no idea how to die. Nothing we have given ourselves to has prepared us for this threshold. We have no control over what greets us on the other side. Our life has been built on us, and it is frightening to stand on the edge of our existence...alone.

But what if life now is simply a prelude? What if the real concerto is being played in the world beyond death? What if in fact the notion of death is a misnomer, and death in this reality is simply the doorway to the next?

What if life has very little to do with you, yet everything to do with God? What if mercy was freely offered, abundant and free? What if you didn't have to earn it, and regardless of how you used it, it was offered again...and again...and again? What if God really wanted you to know Him? What if you could still walk in the cool of the afternoon with the Creator?

You can.

Whether you started your journey with God long ago and find yourself needing to be reminded of the truest things, eternal things, or whether you are just beginning to consider your spiritual life, let me remind you of a God who waits. He waits for you. He waits with arms full of mercy.

So, learn to live—truly live—and when the time comes, you will also know how to die. The realities of both the here and the hereafter flow from the wounds of a Savior who died to offer you everything you need: Himself, and the mercy only He offers, mercy necessary for this life and the next.

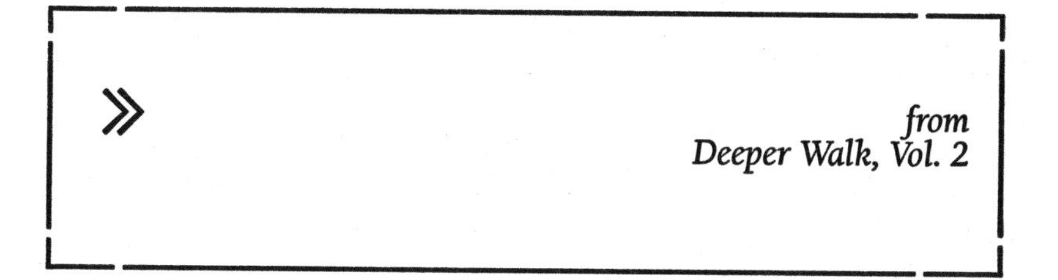

Winn Collier is a writer and a pastor of a university church, Downtown Community Fellowship, in Clemson, SC.

A Modern Day Prodigal

By Winn Collier

The Gospel is for sinners. Sounds simple—a review of fourth grade Sunday school material leaping from the flannel graph. However, I sense it is time for a return to the most fundamental of Christian truths: the Gospel.

In the Gospel, we find hurting, scabbed over, sinful, self-willed, arrogant, rebellious, lonely wrecks offered hope and the very life of God. What we desperately needed, He became for us...and in us. Few would disagree. Unfortunately, however, we normally view all this in the past tense. We look back at the Gospel. The Gospel isn't just the initial message prompting us onto the path of God's kingdom. The Gospel is what we need every moment of our existence, each baby step down the path.

Reviewing the story of the prodigal, the abrupt ending is striking. We aren't told how the elder brother responded to his father's tender request he join the celebration and surrender his bitter self-righteousness. The "dark character" in the parable's plot had been the younger son whose greed had shamed himself, his father, and his family. However, the story ends with an unanticipated turn: The younger son is broken in His Father's arms while the elder son is defiant to His Father's invitation.

The story is left hanging, and amazingly, the elder son becomes the "dark character," brooding outside the party of forgiveness. This craftily turned climax must have disturbed the Pharisees as they recognized Jesus identifying them with the elder brother. The elder brother was disgusted with the father's affection for his wayward son, and the Pharisees would have joined that disgust.

Jesus aimed to challenge their pretentious righteousness. In scorning the prodigal's return, on some levels they became him.

Which sin is worse? Leaving the father...or refusing the father? Some prodigals sin "big" and then wake up from their foolishness. Some prodigals sin "little" and stand just outside the embrace of grace.

Many have been radically changed by grace. We are amazed by it...drawn to it...overwhelmed by it...incredibly thankful for it. However, we may need to come to a new place: the realization that we need it. It is proper to be thankful for the heart of the gracious father in the story of the prodigal sons. In this new place, though, we see ourselves in the story: we are the prodigals. The Gospel is for prodigals. Like us.

EVEN DEEPER

Sit down with the story in Luke 15. Ask yourself which character you are. How do you need to come home?

PRAYER

Gracious Father, I have wandered from You. Sometimes I wander in open rebellion, relishing sin rather than You. God, I need the Gospel. I need it each time I see my sin, and even more when I don't. I am a prodigal. Help me to run with reckless abandon, home to You.

»

from
Deeper Walk, Vol. 2

Winn Collier is a writer and a pastor of a university church, Downtown Community Fellowship, in Clemson, SC.

A Holy Tasting

By Winn Collier

Recently I have explored the discipline of Lectio Divina, an ancient devotional practice that emerged in the early days of the church and was nurtured along the centuries by the Benedictine movement. Lectio Divina is Latin for holy reading, and it offers an invitation to hear the voice of God arise out of the Scriptures.

Steeped in technical, literal—almost scientific—exegesis of Scripture, it can be difficult to move past analyzing God's Word and deeper into the unhurried art of listening to it. Lectio Divina is not antithetical to sound interpretation of the text's meaning, but it does challenge the sad reality that technical interpretation can often become our god. We seize God's words, but we miss God's heart.

Quieting our mind, engaging our spirit, being moved by more than sentence structure and original meanings—why are these simple-sounding notions so rare to experience? Why is connecting our heart with God's such a struggle?

Could it be due to our loss of the art of savoring, our loss of the pleasure of taste? Listening to God's heart belongs to the realm of beauty—the world of experience, image, and taste. We often live in the realm of science—the world of exactness, logic, and duty.

We are a people of solutions. Give us a problem, and we'll fix it. Offer a question, and we'll find an answer. We are an efficient, self-achieving, driven band. There is little room for ambiguity, little space for pondering, and only rare moments to pause, breathe deeply, and wonder if there could be more to our restless wanderings than a slavish quest for the holy grail—getting it right. Unfortunately, getting it right plays no part in experiencing beauty.

In the heart-tugging movie, *Kate and Leopold*, Leopold is a royal duke transplanted through a time portal from 1876 into the present. The quirky plot is the budding romance between a successful modern woman and...well...a duke from 1876. Far more interesting than the main storyline, however, is the sub-plot: Leopold's attempts to come to terms with life in the modern age. The world he left has vanished, and he isn't certain he likes what is in its place. In one poignant scene, Leopold's frustrated observation is telling: "Life is not solely composed of tasks, but tastes." And he is right.

If our heart has chilled, the voice of God grown distant, perhaps we need space to savor. The psalmist knew this and offered this invitation: "Taste and see that the Lord is good" (PSALM 34:8).

EVEN DEEPER

Meditate on Psalm 63. Savor God. Enjoy a sunset. Take a walk in the woods.

PRAYER

Beautiful One, help me to taste You, to breathe You.

»

from
Deeper Walk, Vol. 2

Winn Collier is a writer and a pastor of a university church, Downtown Community Fellowship, in Clemson, SC.

In Between

By Margaret Feinberg

» There's a place between here and there. A piece of ground in the middle of take-off and landing. A section of the unknown within beginning and ending. You probably find yourself there from time to time. It's the land known as Inbetween.

Inbetween is one of the most rugged places in life. You aren't fully here, and you aren't fully there. Your emotions and hopes are strewn across an endless list of possibilities. Door knobs of wood, brass, and silver line the path, but which will open? In the land of Inbetween, the paths are lined with sealed envelopes and foggy dreams. Excitement runs forward and fears hold back. And if you stay long enough, you feel the tremors of your soul.

The land of Inbetween is downright scary. It's a place of blind trust. It's where the pedals of faith meet the narrow road of fortitude and where movement is demanded though there's no place to go. The worst part about this land isn't the uncertainty or frustration that accompany it—it's that God likes it when you're there.

While He's no sadist, God loves the land of Inbetween. He loves what it does to us. He loves the humility and dependence it creates in our hearts, so He creates innumerable forks in life's road that swerve us into the land of Inbetween. The unknowns of job, marriage, children, and home are the road signs of this uncertain land. At times, people are thrust into Inbetween by mishaps, accidents, sudden deaths, and even unexpected fortune. Some people visit so many times they begin to wonder if it's life. And they aren't far off.

So what will hold you steady when you walk through the terrain of Inbetween? A recognition that Inbetween is God's design. In one miraculous moment, the Creator of the universe placed you in the greatest Inbetween of all time—the place between this earthy creation and eternity. Life's smaller lunges forward and backward are merely postcard reminders that there's something greater than this place we're visiting.

If you're in your own land of Inbetween, remember that God was the original designer of this journey. You can get mad, scream and even pout if you want. But it doesn't change the fact that you're merely passing through. Everything else is Inbetween.

EVEN DEEPER

Read about the stages of Israel's journey in Numbers 33, then draw a time line of your life. Mark significant dates on it. Reflect on how far God has brought you. Ponder Psalm 23:4.

PRAYER

Father, my heart longs for eternity but my body remains here. Help me to see life as a journey that is completed through communion with You.

»

from
Deeper Walk, Vol. 1

Margaret Feinberg is a writer based in Steamboat Springs, Colorado. She has written for a variety of nationally recognized magazines and is a contributing writer to *Enjoying God* and *I AM RELEVANT.*

Bored with God

By Winn Collier

The adjective I could often use for my spiritual life is numb. Such a description doesn't conjure up images of spiritual heroics, but there is a certain noble ring to it.

A weary warrior halts and crouches; in a daze, he scans the charred battlefield. Numb. A grief-stricken woman battles deep loss in the caverns of her soul. Numb. We are often numb because we have fought well. We are weary. Tired. Numb. And that actually sounds pretty valiant.

Unfortunately, however, at times what I really feel is nothing so gallant as numbness. I face a much darker reality. I am bored with God.

You have been there—you want to pursue the Almighty, but all you can manage is a yawn. You take a walk to pray, and the slightest distraction pulls you from the Throne. You plan to use the quiet of your commute to commune with God; and within seconds, everything within you wants to flip on the radio. You don't care if all you can pick up is static—you just need the noise. You can't stand the quiet. It's boring. Bored with God.

Lord Byron seemed to think boredom an inevitable element of proper society: "Society is now one polish'd horde, formed of two mighty tribes, the Bores and Bored." So, is that how it is? Boredom is inevitable? Just accept it? Bury it, and play the game, pretending your spiritual life runs deep so others won't notice the coldness swallowing your heart?

Boredom may prove inevitable, but it isn't God's design. Jesus said He can live with His followers being hot or cold, but the mucky middle of lukewarm is where the stench brews. Boredom is a polite term for the stench of being unmoved by the grandeur of God.

Boredom reveals something deeper: our hearts have been captured by something other than God. The proper response is not to do more, work harder, or make more commitments. These aren't responses of the heart. The result of endless activity for God is boredom—He has become small, replaced by a focus on our efforts.

We need to reconnect with the romancing God whose story ignites our imagination. We must allow time and space to simply be creatures of our God, listening to His story afresh, sitting at His feet anew, and quieting our hearts in His presence. In time, a fresh awakening will yield. And as we struggle to find words to describe this awakening, boredom won't even be considered.

EVEN DEEPER

Study Romans 12:11-13. What adjectives describe your spiritual life? Write down four or five.

PRAYER

God of Wonder, allow me to be quiet and see You afresh.
Capture my heart.

» *from*
Deeper Walk, Vol. 1

Winn Collier is a writer and a pastor of a university church, Downtown Community Fellowship, in Clemson, SC.

A Psalm

By Alecia Stephens

» I praise you, Lord God, that You are the great Artist and that creation is Your canvas. As a painter steps back and sighs in contentment at his finished work, so You delight in the beauty You have created by Your good pleasure.

I see how You have carved the valleys out of mountains like a sculptor. Each crevice and cliff has a place in your grand design, and as I look down upon Your work, I see that each crevice and cliff creates a breathless scene. Every waterfall that flows down from the mountains replenishes Your work. I stand at the bottom of the rushing waters and feel the cool mist upon my face. I see dozens of rainbows before the falls and agree that Your creation is good.

I stand at the base of the granite peaks, in wonder of their mass. I grow aware of how small I am compared to the Creator and Artist. I wonder how You can ever notice me in the vastness of Your work?

I hear the music You make in the roar of the waterfalls, in the bird's song, in the hush of the breeze through the green meadows, and most of all in the silence.

I love the colors of the flowers You created. Many artists try to capture the hues You have mixed, but none compare with Your design. Your have saved your most beautiful colors for the sunset, painting the gray, rocky peaks in their shades.

I believe You greatly rejoice in bathing your creation with the light of the moon. You take pleasure in my gaping over the beauty. I know You have created the multitude of stars, hanging them in place.

I see this art and am drawn to the Artist. It is He who formed the masterpiece, and it is He who holds it together. And I cannot help but praise the Creator.

EVEN DEEPER

Revisit the account of creation in Genesis 1, 2. Take some time to go to the mountains, the beach, or even a park in your town, and spend time praising God for His creation.

PRAYER

I thank You, Lord, that Your beauty is all around me.
Help me to see the works of Your hand.

» *from*
Deeper Walk, Vol. 1

Authors are freelance writers to RELEVANTmagazine.com in an ongoing series called *Deeper Walk*. They're a mix of writers as diverse as our audience: professional writers, pastors, college students, stay-at-home moms, and business professionals.

Drawing Close

By Derek MacLeod

In our quest for efficiency, we punch out emails quickly to friends and colleagues. Avoiding the words that would take too long to spell, we write in a smooth, brisk fashion. At times I find myself applying this same "quick, get it over and done with" attitude to my time with God.

I recently felt the effects of my briskness with God. I was distant in my prayer time, scattered in my attempts to worship. Prayer was more of a checklist than a conversation. Pondering over my plight, I realized the unthinkable: I was ignoring God.

We often think of God as "detached." He's over there, and we're over here. We are mistaken. God is with us. He is around us. He covers us. He aches when we ignore Him, too busy for our God. Yet He remains faithful. He is just, jealous, angry, compassionate, and merciful. He longs for us, our companionship, our fellowship. He longs for our love.

We can't simply turn God on and off. We can't ignore Him and then expect to experience His nearness whenever we feel the urge. All relationships in the human dimension require love, care, and attention. They require time. Relationships in the spiritual dimension are no different. God is near. God is ready. God is waiting.

"Because of the Lord's great love we are not consumed, for his compassions never fail. They are new every morning; great is your faithfulness. I say to myself, 'The Lord is my portion; therefore I will wait for him'" (Lamentations 3:22-24).

The Lord waits for our unending worship. Sit down with Him.

Go for a walk with Him; listen to Him. Take your relationship deeper and develop a treasured closeness to your Maker.

EVEN DEEPER

James 4:8 says, "Come near to God and he will come near to you." Find a place where you can meet God and set aside time solely for that purpose. God will meet with you.

PRAYER

Lord, it amazes me that You want to spend time with me. Forgive me for ignoring You. Place in my heart an eagerness to meet You and enjoy Your glorious presence.

»

from
Deeper Walk, Vol. 1

Authors are freelance writers to RELEVANTmagazine.com in an ongoing series called *Deeper Walk*. They're a mix of writers as diverse as our audience: professional writers, pastors, college students, stay-at-home moms, and business professionals.

ALL DAY

BY WINN COLLIER

»Dawn. Awake. Crisp. Air. Rested. Birds. Chirp. Dew. Alive. Dog. Out. Run. Newspaper. Coffee. Shower. Sing. Pray. Sing. Shave. Nick. Bagel. Oranges. Wheaties.

Kiss. Kids. Lunchboxes. Kiss. School. Briefcase. Commute. Radio. News. Noise. Honk. Reports. Meetings. Coffee. Spill. Laugh. Argue. Create. Confront. Joke. Appointment. Lunch. Sandwich. Salad. Pie. No. Fruit. Office.

Midday. Phone. Conference. Call. Scribble. E-mail.

Fax. Pager. Deadline. Wired. Wireless. Headset. Pace. Wrangle. Buy. Sell. Trade. Tylenol. Interrupt. Call. Home. Smile. Love. Truth. Good. God. Commute. Store. Forget. Return. Store. Traffic. Radio. News. Noise. Horn. Home. Kids. Run. Jump. Play. Wrestle. Laugh. Remember.

Dusk. Crickets. Chirp. Sky. Orange. Breeze. Streetlights. Flicker. Dinner. Family. Laugh. Highchair. Spill. Laugh. Mop. Ice Cream. Yes. Chocolate. Vanilla. Strawberry. Mom. Dad. Walk. Twilight. Talk. Hands. Share. Laugh. Remember. Kids. Bed. Up. Bed. Drink. Bed. Monsters. Bed. Hushed. Quiet. Kisses. Rest. Good. God. Good.

"From the rising of the sun to its setting, the name of the Lord is to be praised" (PSALM 113:3 NAS).

EVEN DEEPER

Write a few words that describe the flow of your day. How can these lead you to worship God? Study Psalm 113:3.

PRAYER

God of the rising and the setting sun, I want to experience you in the midst of the day, throughout it, and intertwined with it. Don't allow me to be content to just give you portions of it. I want all of You in all of me.

»

Winn Collier is a writer and a pastor of a university church, Downtown Community Fellowship, in Clemson, SC.

Cultivating Intimacy

By S. J. Hill

» How do you practice the presence of God when you first get up in the morning feeling like a zombie? How do you go from school, a busy work environment, the mall, or the gym to waiting on God? If you find it difficult, then you're normal. Waking up in the morning and not feeling much of anything won't inspire you to seek the Father. Having to leave your fast-paced lifestyle long enough to meet with Him is also far from easy. We've been culturally conditioned to live with constant busyness, noise, and activity.

Transitioning into a time of intimacy is often difficult. The mind races. The to-do list grows. And often, a little demonic voice whispers, "You're just wasting your time."

But waiting on God is essential. It's worth the effort. Hebrews 4:1 challenges us not to fall short of entering into His rest. He promises that rest can come to our hearts as we are intimate with Him. But the rest that accompanies intimacy isn't an absence of discipline. Verse 11 of the same chapter admonishes us to "...labour therefore to enter into that rest..." (KJV). Resting in intimacy with the Father is the fruit of consistent discipline. It isn't about being regimented or legalistic. It's about continually stirring ourselves up to seek the Lord. It's bringing our hearts and minds into a position to commune with Him.

So on a practical level, how do we do it?

One of the most effective ways to cultivate your relationship with the Father is to have a place that the two of you can call your own. It can be a place in your home—a certain room or place on the couch or the floor. It can be outdoors as well. A nearby wooded area, stream, open field, path, or street can become your place. Whatever the location, it needs to be an area where you can go just to be with Him.

Jesus had His favorite places in which to seek His Father. Luke 22:39 says, "Jesus went out as usual to the Mount of Olives, and his disciples followed him." It's clear that the Mount of Olives was a key place for Jesus in cultivating intimacy with His Father. As I've studied the lives of great saints, I've become even more convinced that each of us needs a special place of retreat, so that when we come into that place, it will automatically remind us of why we're there.

»A PLACE FOR INTIMACY

Once you retreat to the place that belongs to the two of you, you're going to need something to help calm your mind and emotions. You're going to find that your mind will be thinking about all the activities of the upcoming day or it will still be racing from all the events of the past few hours. Often a small to-do list will begin building in your mind. In order to remove this distraction, keep a piece of paper and a pen nearby. Record the things you need to do on the paper so that your heart and mind will be free to pursue God.

One of the best things you can do is listen to good worship music. Some of you may prefer to play your guitar or the piano. Do whatever works for you. Music helps me focus on the Father. Even taking walks with Him helps me unwind from the events of the day. I love being outside! The important thing is to find something that will help calm your heart and mind and assist you in transitioning from life's racetrack to God's resting place.

You may also want to prayerfully ask the Father to help you in this matter. You can pray something like this: "Father, settle my mind so I can meditate on Your heart and Your holy purposes. Give me the grace during this time to focus my passions and my emotions on You. Father, remove the yokes of this world, and yoke me to

Your eternal purposes. Energize me. Let this time be rich. I'm here to meet with You. Invade the recesses of my heart, and help me stay focused on You. Manifest Yourself to me, not only in this place, but also throughout the rest of the day. In Jesus' name."

As your mind begins to unwind, start to express words of love and adoration to the Father. You can do it out loud or under your breath. Your words don't have to be complex or even complete sentences. Express your heart to Him. Tell Him what you like about Him. Thank Him for the little things He's done in your life. As you worship, remember that He's not out there somewhere in the wild blue yonder. He lives inside you. Your body is His temple. Offer yourself as a resting place for Him, and tell Him that you want Him to be your resting place.

Eventually your mind and emotions will cooperate, and you'll be able to focus on the Father. How busy your day is or how hectic your day has already been may determine how quickly you can bring your mind into an attitude of worship. Be patient. Continue seeking Him. Remember, He rewards those who earnestly seek Him (HEB. 11:6). It takes time to cultivate intimacy with the Father. But He's longing for fellowship with you as well. And He's not giving up any time soon, so neither should you.

Try to find times throughout the day to steal away with Him. In other words, run away with Him in your heart and mind while you're driving to and from work, riding in an elevator, waiting in the grocery checkout line, or working out on a treadmill. The Father is everywhere, and His desire for you is unending. Bring your thoughts around to Him throughout the day. Express your love and adoration. Ask Him to bring you into a deeper awareness of His presence until you find yourself living more and more in an attitude of prayer and worship.

»PRAYERFUL MEDITATION

Why do you read the Bible? Is it something you feel you're obligated to do before you can begin your day or turn off the lights at night? Meditating on the Word isn't about reading a certain number of verses or chapters in the Bible every day. Neither is it merely educational. While a systematic study of the Bible is a wonderful and necessary part of the Christian life, reflecting on the Scriptures isn't about gaining information—it's about transformation. If you want your times in the Word to truly change you, then you can't read the Bible like a textbook or the latest novel. You can't race through the Word and expect nuggets of truth to leap off the pages at you.

Meditating on the Word isn't meant to be an achievement—it's meant to be an experience. There may be times when you don't get beyond two or three verses. But don't let that bother you. Just as a passing glance at a beautiful painting will never be sufficient to reveal its secrets, speed-reading the Bible will never be rewarding. Like a great painting, the Word must be savored and absorbed in the depths of your heart. Reflecting on the Scriptures involves not only your mind but also your whole being. A person who truly meditates on the Word doesn't merely think about what he's reading. He experiences it!

I love meditating on the Scriptures. I love taking the Word and rolling it over and over in my mind, allowing it to bathe my heart and emotions. I enjoy picturing myself in the stories and taking in all the sights and sounds of the moment. I love reflecting on the Psalms until they become as personal as my own thoughts and feelings.

I also enjoy praying the Scriptures back to the Father as I allow the words to express the cry of my heart. For example, in Psalm 119:18, David prayed, "Open my eyes that I may see wonderful things in your law." Over the years, I have made this my prayer as well. This has been my approach as I've meditated on the Word. After a time of worship, when my mind and emotions are focused on the Father, I ask Him to make His Word come alive in my heart. I pray for Him to open my spiritual eyes so I can behold His beauty through the Scriptures. I remind myself continually that the Father has left me some inspiring love letters so I can know and love Him more intimately.

In your quest to cultivate intimacy with the Father, I also highly recommend journaling. I'm not talking about recording the events of the day but writing honestly and deeply about the things you feel the Holy Spirit is speaking to your heart. Write about your struggles as well as your victories. Give yourself the chance to ask some hard questions. Journaling should be reflective and an honest expression of your heart. Journaling will allow you to get in touch with your deepest feelings.

Another method for cultivating intimacy with God is the practice of silence. The Father is continually whispering to us, "Be still, and know that I am God" (Ps. 46:10). However, the idea is foreign to most of us. The thought of being silent unnerves us.

I remember the first time I tried to practice silence. I just about went nuts. I was the kind of person who always had to be around people. But the more I waited on the Lord, the easier it became. I now love to sit in the Father's presence. I love to focus on Him and allow Him to settle on me and speak to me.

Remember, it's His nature to manifest Himself. He wants to be with you even more than you want to be with Him. He wants to speak to you. Open your heart to Him. Begin with short periods of time. Don't say anything. Just focus on the One who lives inside you. Reflect on the beauty of His heart. Contemplate His greatness. Occasionally, you can whisper some words of love and devotion to Him. But the purpose of silence is to allow Him to settle on you and bathe you in His peace and love. Your heart was made for this.

The more you cultivate this aspect of communion with the Father, the easier it will become. It may be difficult at first, but you will eventually cherish it.

As I've shared my heart with you about cultivating intimacy with the Father, I want you to understand that these are just suggestions to help you in your journey. I don't always do the same things every day, and I want you to feel free to be creative as you seek the Father. Don't do anything based on duty alone. Learn to delight in the Lover of your heart. As a friend of mine always says, "It's going from 'got to' to 'get to.'" It isn't about doing something just because it's the Christian thing to do. It's all about relationship. We get to enjoy the Father. We get to rest in His love and feel the pleasure of His heart.

The Father is also looking for a resting place. "This is what the Lord says: 'Heaven is my throne, and the earth is my footstool. Where is the house you will build for me? Where will my resting place be?'" (ISA. 66:1). Does the Father have a resting place in your life?

A pastor from Argentina once told me about several unbelievers who were walking down the sidewalk in front of a church in his city. The congregation was experiencing a real move of the Spirit of God. As these people walked past the Church, they were overwhelmed by the presence of the Lord. They found themselves on the ground, unable to move. Several believers saw them and carried them into the building, where they eventually were saved. Although this story may seem a bit outlandish, it made me realize just how much God jealously longs for a people in which to live. He is looking for a resting place in the hearts of men. I believe we're coming into a season of time when the Father is going to reveal Himself in such a way that He will capture the heart of a generation.

I want you to be a part of that. Open your heart to Him. Let Him sweep you off your feet by ravishing you with His beauty. Let Him captivate you with His fiery passion. He wants to be your heart's delight. He wants you to enjoy Him forever.

»CLOSING PRAYER

Father, open my heart to the fullness of knowing You. Create in me a hunger and desire to seek You. I want to be a passionate lover. Help me to go deeper with You in all areas of my life. Remove the distractions. Remove the hindrances. Remove the things that stand between us so I can run after You with wholehearted abandonment.

I want to live for You. I love You. Mold me. Shape me. Form me. And carry me in the palm of Your hand so I may enjoy You forever. In Jesus' name.

»

from
Enjoying God

S.J. Hill is a Bible teacher, speaker and author. He is currently on staff at Mike Bickle's Forerunner School of Prayer and is professor emeritus at F.I.R.E. School of Ministry and has previously authored two books.

Why We're Bored with Worship

By Winn Collier

Worship has never had it so good. The vocabulary of worship has become mainstream in religious culture, and worship leaders are in high demand. Churches are investing hundreds of thousands of dollars in state-of-the-art equipment, cranking it up in theater style "worship centers," renovated warehouses and mainline cathedrals. Jumbo screens, candles, art, global tunes, banners and aesthetic sensitivity are just a few of the elements infused into the exploding worship rage.

Reacting against old forms and dispassionate, formalistic worship, a wave of renewal has morphed into a monsoon. Rightly responding to a creative God, the church has erupted with diversity. Whether one prefers worship from the Celts of the Emerald Isle, the raw throbs from the underground culture, Gregorian chants or any variation of classic hymns, it is available. The church has sought to create energy and momentum with limitless options and exceptional quality.

And it's working. Worship bands pack out major venues, and CD sales are soaring. A recent recording executive alluded to the big business of worship, noting that approximately one out of every four albums they bring to the Christian market are of the worship genre.

More telling is that most church vision statements refer to a core value of worship. The landscape of the worshiping church has shifted. Our vocabulary, practice, and theology have radically evolved. Worship is hip. Worshiping is in vogue.

Yet some are warning all is not well. The obvious concern of worship as business is often raised. Darin Sasser of the worship band Among Thorns said, "It's tough…because this worship thing is really on the rise...You have to let people understand that you're not just doing this for a buck—you sincerely want to lead them in an intimate worship experience with God."

The marketing of worship has raised more than a few eyebrows. Matt Redman responded to one such scheme: "I saw a U.S. worship album recently subtitled *America's Ten Most Powerful Worship Songs*. Who told them that—God?…It made me giggle, but it also made me concerned. That sort of marketing shows we easily lose the plot if we're not careful."

But even more disconcerting is that for all our creativity, diversity, quality and capital investment, we are fundamentally still unmoved. Our worship may be exciting, but we, as worshipers, are still bored. It seems we possess the ingredients for life-altering worship, but the growing reality is that ingredients aren't enough. Why are we bored with encountering the Almighty?

Ancient voices often provide the clearest illumination for our modern moments of darkness. The Canticles emerged from the medieval church as prayers offered in a 30-day cycle, intended to be prayed each day of the month. The purpose is to reorient our days to the rhythms of God, placing us humbly at His feet. In one collection, the first line of the first canticle reads, "O all you works of God." The starting point of a month of prayers reminds us we are God's work. We are His. I suspect our worship lacks fervent life because we have lost the core theme of Christian theology: Everything is for God. Everything.

The mystics called it "centering on God." The reformers spoke of "God's providence." Modern prophets plead that we return to the "centrality of God." These voices blend into an ominous harmony, drawing attention to a somber reality: God is small to us.

Somehow amid our activity of worship, we have forgotten the plot. Maybe it would better to say we have forgotten the central character. Scripture speaks of worship as the dwelling place of the triune God, but sadly it is often treated solely as the domain of man.

Subtly, worship has been reduced because it has come to be viewed *primarily* as the activity of man directed toward God. Certainly, worship is a heart-stirred sacrifice we offer our Creator. But we often miss where worship originates. Worship begins with the activity of God.

Worship is woven into our DNA. God created us for worship. Alexander Schmemann defined secularism as "above all a negation of worship...not of God's existence [but of] man as a worshiping being, as *homo adorans*." We had nothing to do with this inbred yearning. It is God's handiwork. Worship isn't our idea, some "goodie" we give to God for giving us what we want. Worship is God's idea.

Our experiences of worship are simply singular moments in the eternal symphony of worship. God has been bringing glory to Himself since before humanity stepped on the earth, and God will bring glory to Himself beyond the end of human days. Genesis begins with God gathering worshipers from the dust of the earth, and Revelation ends with God reveling in the climactic worship of all the nations. God takes pleasure in our adoration, but He doesn't need us. Our worship isn't the central plot. We aren't the central character. God is.

Many view worship as an activity or emotion we stir up as an act of gratitude to God. While gratitude is a noble and necessary response to God, such a perspective again shifts the focus from God to us. As the Christian Reformed Church report on worship offered: "It is tempting to think of the people, the worshipers, as the ones who make worship happen...God is the one who always has initiated the relationship between God and his people."

If worship is primarily something we make happen, then worship is centered on us. If worship is centered on us, it is small—God is small.

And this small God is one we use for our own devices. Worship becomes centrally what we "feel," what we "want," the style we "like." We race after worship experiences like addicts race after the back alley crack dealer. Rather than being captured by the Eternal One, we simply use His name for an emotional high. We view God as the one enabling us to "enjoy worship," another perk from the endless giver of good things. We miss the audience of our worship. We forget we stand on holy ground in His presence. We forget we were created for His glory, not Him for ours. The god we worship is one of our own making, and nothing could be more boring than that.

The Psalmist has a knack for making an ordinary—almost trite—remark blaze with fresh reality. In Psalm 104, the writer offers a plain observation, serving to reorient our very existence, "O Lord my God, you are *very great.*" Small gods are not great. Small gods do not evoke worship. Small gods yield boredom.

Perhaps it is time to return to simpler things, to ancient wisdom. Might it be time to give God center stage again? Maybe rather than seeking an experience, a moment or a certain ecstatic ambiance, we could again become simple seekers of God, the Great One.

We may be coming to this table late, but thankfully centuries of the church before us have followed a God-centered existence. Historically, the church has kept God central by living out the drama of God. This was reflected in the way they ordered their community's life, telling God's story in history through the liturgical calendar (Advent, Christmas, Epiphany, Lent, etc.). They furthered this by the oral traditions where story was valued above principles. The acts of the communal spiritual life, shared meals and common prayers flamed a passionate life, ordered by the presence of a mighty God. Worship was simple, but God loomed large.

Perhaps we could return to our roots. Perhaps God could loom large among us again. Approaching worship as a response to the initiation of God rather than something we "work up" for Him might help. We could see our expressions of worship as simply one more stone in the altar of sacrifice God's people have been building for millennia. We could abandon the stifling pull to be chic and trendy, allowing creativity to emerge from our identity as God's image bearers rather than from the man-centered addiction to something "new."

We could gather to pray—pray simple prayers. We could live out our prayers and our worship by seeing the connection between acts of compassion on Tuesday and voices lifted to God on Sunday. We could pursue community more intentionally, believing worship is not a solitary affair. We could resist the modern urge for everything to move fast, feel good and give us what we demand. We could leave room for ambiguity, mystery, loneliness, disappointment and quiet. We could leave room for God.

Worship is simply ordering our life in such a way that we reflect back to Him His great worth. As William Temple observed, "To worship is to quicken the conscience by the holiness of God, to feed the mind with the truth of God, to purge the imagination by the beauty of God, to open the heart to the love of God, to devote the will to the purpose of God." Worship is all about God, a *very great* God. A big God. How did we miss it?

While such a God would not fit well within much of our structured confines, refusing to jump into place at 10 a.m. on Sunday, He would not be small. He certainly would not be boring.

Perhaps our boredom with worship is a good thing. Perhaps we are growing bored with ourselves.

»

from
RELEVANT magazine

Winn Collier is a writer and a pastor of a university church, Downtown Community Fellowship, in Clemson, SC.

I LOVE GOD, BUT I HATE YOU

BY CHRIS SEAY

I was driving to the Phoenix airport on Sept. 11 as tragedy polluted our lives with anxiety and deep sadness. The cross-country drive home to Texas was laced with horrific anticipation that more tragedy at the hands of Islamic extremists was around the corner.

But Islam is not the only religion with hateful manifestations. Christianity bears the scars of the Crusades, holocaust of Jews, slavery, prejudice and, it seems, a continued hostility toward culture on the whole. Watching Christian leaders speak on television feels like a full contact sport. They start talking, and I feel like I just got kicked in the gut.

Like a bleeding soldier, our nation's wounds were exposed when Jerry Falwell went on the *700 Club* and doused them with salt saying, "God continues to lift the curtain and allow the enemies of America to give us probably what we deserve. The American Civil Liberties Union has got to take a lot of blame for this."

Then Falwell broadened his blast to include the federal courts and others who he said were "throwing God out of the public square." He added, "The abortionists have got to bear some burden for this because God will not be mocked. And when we destroy 40 million little innocent babies, we make God mad. I really believe that the pagans, and the abortionists, and the feminists, and the gays and the lesbians who are actively trying to make that an alternative lifestyle, the ACLU, People for the American Way—all of them who have tried to secularize America—I point the finger in their face and say, 'You helped this happen.'"

Who could even defend the rantings of the media-driven fundamentalist?

In Houston during a protest over insurance for partners of gay city employees, Grace Baptist Church Pastor Aubrey Vaughn looked straight in the *Fox News* camera and said, "Those sodomites should have 'em an island. They got plenty of money—they ought to buy 'em an island, and every sodomite ought to go out there to that island and just stay there. And maybe we can drop 'em a little food if they don't know how to grow their own food."

I called him the following week at his church to see if he was taken out of context or somehow misspoke. When I asked him if this was his actual statement, Vaughn wanted it to be perfectly clear that the article had left something out. In his plan, those sodomites would have to pay for any food dropped to them (they don't get no charity).

Then Vaughn informed me that the Bible calls sodomy an abomination, and Asa removed all sodomites from the community. When asked about the importance of living under the Hebrew Law of the Old Testament, he said, "We must live under the whole Law!"

After further interrogation, Vaughn confessed to wearing shirts made of two different kinds of thread, in his case a blend of cotton and polyester (mostly polyester), which is expressly forbidden in Leviticus 19:19. He also makes a habit of shaking the hands of women without asking if they are currently menstruating (Leviticus 15:19-24), a flagrant violation of the law. Furthermore, he partakes of shellfish of all kinds: barbecued shrimp, teriyaki shrimp, coconut shrimp, Creole shrimp, fried shrimp, and even shrimp salad, which the Old Testament considers an abomination (Leviticus 11:10) and requires he be stoned to death. I asked him if we could set an appointment for his stoning. In seeing his own transgression, Vaughn joked that stoning would soon have to become a regular event in his congregation.

This is the beauty of the new story found in Christ. We all should be stoned, but we have been shown grace. Could we try offering some grace to others?

We often bemoan the decline of morality in our land as if we can expect something different from an increasingly post-Christian population. I am not an ambassador for morality, and I do not long to see the world become a more moral place. I want to see people come to faith in God, and only after they have come to faith will they see their entire lives transformed. We have made it very clear in the area of the city we work in that we are not against homosexuality. Our mission is not to see people leave homosexual lifestyles but for men and women to experience the freeing Gospel of Jesus Christ.

The Church should refocus on the Gospel instead of the culture wars. It is to our shame that we point out sin to our culture knowing that without the power of Christ, they are ill-equipped to see their lives change. Instead, let us speak the love of Christ by loving all people. The Apostle Paul made it very clear that you can do good things, even great things, but if you have not love, it is useless. Jesus said, "Others will know you follow me if you love one another" (JOHN 13:35). A life of real faith is marked by love.

My sacred text, the Bible, says: "We love because he first loved us. If anyone says, 'I love God,' yet hates his brother, he is a liar. For anyone who does not love his brother, whom he has seen, cannot love God, whom he has not seen. And he has given us this command: Whoever loves God must also love his brother" (1 JOHN 4:19-21).

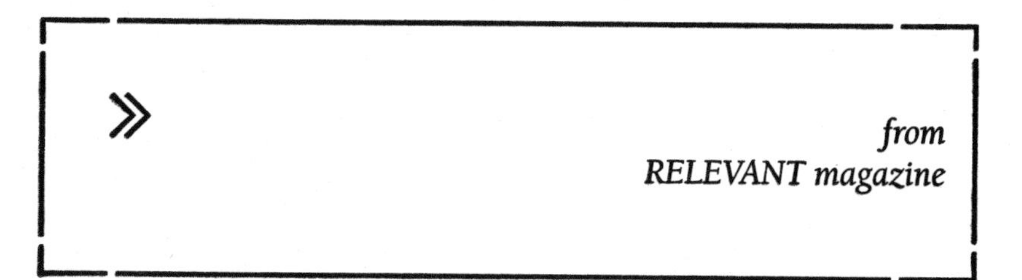

Chris Seay, author of *The Gospel According to Tony Soprano*, is currently pastor of Ecclesia, a progressive Christian community in Houston, Texas, where he lives with his wife and three young daughters.

Not Just Here In America

By John Fischer

In all my thinking, writing and speaking on the Christian subculture in America, I have always assumed at least one thing: The phenomenon of a Christian subculture and its accompanying errors and blind spots only exist in America. Surely this separation of Christian and secular is unknown in other places in the world where regular people can be Christians and have a quiet, steady impact on their culture through normal channels of life and influence without getting caught in the crossfire of a cultural Christian guerilla warfare with all its accompanying socio-political alignments and agendas.

I had this assumption shattered recently while talking with a college senior who grew up as a missionary kid in Guatemala and will be returning there to begin an Internet consulting business upon his graduation. When I asked him how he felt about going, he had very mixed feelings. He was excited about the challenge and the fact that he felt God had opened up a door of opportunity for him there, but he was also very reluctant about it. When I pressed him about the reluctance, he revealed his major concern was having to contend with the fundamentalist evangelical Christian subculture in Guatemala.

"You've got to be kidding," I said. "Not in Guatemala."

"Oh yes," he replied. "It's worse than here."

He went on to tell me how his struggles with the Christian subculture and its accompanying isolationist and separatist beliefs almost did in his own faith growing up as the son of missionary parents there. That's how we became acquainted, actually—through one of my earlier books, which he credits for preserving his faith when he was almost ready to leave it for all the wrong reasons.

Apparently, we have not only exported our faith as missionaries but our bad ideas as well. That means the Christian market is international, and the Christian subculture is a force to be reckoned with worldwide. I guess I shouldn't be surprised. Television, film and music have exported American values throughout the world. Why not Christian television and Christian movies, books and music exporting the thinking and values of a Christian subculture?

It is interesting to note how my friend was hesitant to return to Guatemala because of this. For some time I've been wondering if the day would come when, in order to truly minister the Gospel of Jesus to people, one would have to disassociate oneself from organized and institutional religion of all kinds. Perhaps that time is already here. For all intents and purposes, it is here for my friend, who told me this is precisely why he is returning to the country of his origin as a businessman and not a missionary.

He is also careful to note that he is not an undercover missionary. He's not disguising his missionary zeal and intent. He's simply taking his newly acquired business expertise where he knows it will have a good chance of success. He is going to begin a business, and his ministry will not be any more or less a part of who he is than it would be for any Christian, anywhere. You could say we are all undercover agents for God, but that is only a way of looking at our God-given place in the world where we live out our faith. It is not an agenda.

Some in the non-Christian media are beginning to recognize a covert proselytizing tactic at work among evangelical Christians, especially in Muslim oriented nations. An intercepted memo within *TIME*'s network of journalists shows the magazine at work on a major piece about evangelical "special ops" inside Muslim countries. "Often, to avoid detection by authorities, this new breed [of evangelicals] employs a tactic called 'tentmaking' or 'tunneling.' Essentially, this means doing some kind of other work as a cover or pretext, when your real goal is preaching. A healthy handful of schools in the U.S. actually teach such techniques."

I don't believe this is how my friend would view his return to Guatemala. He is going to go primarily as a businessman who happens to be a Christian. He doesn't have a particular Christian agenda driving his return. He is not a missionary in disguise.

I don't believe our work should be a pretext for something else. At the same time, being Christians in places of influence is a big part of God's overall plan for the Church—something we have often overlooked in our attempts to create a separate contemporary Christian culture. But I see this as *His* strategy, not ours. Our responsibility is to do all we do to the glory of God, wherever He puts us.

We are called to be the best at our profession for reasons that have nothing to do with evangelizing. Our motivation should be that which drives us to do everything well to the glory of God. Whatever we do professionally, we do as an end in itself, not as a means to an end. Christians need to be accepted in the workplace at face value for the kind of people they are and the kind of work that they do. Our Christianity and accompanying evangelical fervor is not a "tactic." Our faith, like our work, needs to stand on its own. Our faith infuses our work with meaning, but it stops short of turning it into cover for a covert operation.

Perhaps we need to examine the end goal. Is it to spread Christianity? To defeat Islam? To make converts? Or to glorify God? I believe if we make the latter our goal, we will accomplish the other three in due order.

As Islamic fundamentalism takes on more and more of a militant nature, Christians must beware a similar fundamentalist backlash. Christianity never got anywhere it was supposed to be by force or manipulation. Like Peter loping off a soldier's ear and necessitating Christ's healing touch, we make more work for God when we try and accomplish his goals through our means. Let's find our own work and do it to God's glory, knowing that wherever we are, God will accomplish His work through us as we do.

»

from
RELEVANT magazine

John Fischer is an artist, thinker and communicator driven to create and personally deliver a message of deeper understanding of God, confirming those seeking a faith that intersects the real world. His website is *www.fischtank.com.*

Getting Out of the Faith Ghetto

By Dan Buck

» If I had a video store it would have one section: Movies. I'm not sure what effect that would have on business, but it would certainly reflect a lesson I've been learning and relearning from the moment I began thinking for myself. The lesson is this: Life is one category. It seems simple enough, and hardly Earth-shattering, but as I think about its implications, I find myself awe-struck by the possibilities of a life lived from this mindset.

Do you remember how the books you read in literature courses were always set in a historical context that your English professor often felt inadequate to discuss without the help of a history professor? Have you wandered aimlessly up and down the supermarket aisle designated "Sauces" looking desperately for soy sauce only to discover that it's actually kept in the "Ethnic Foods" aisle? And have you recently noticed that the most casual of conversations with a non-believer has an alienating "spiritual aspect" to it even though you were trying to avoid being too "Christiany"? The reason for all these quandaries is the same: Life is one category.

»God Penciled In

Postmodernism has given a shot in the arm to spirituality, but unfortunately, it has been relegated to a spot in our day timer between a stop at Starbucks and the health club. We have made God a category in our life. And we think we're improving in our walk when we spend more time in that category: "The more often I have morning devotionals, the better Christian I am." And while morning devotionals are important, the truth is your time in Revelation is as spiritual as your chat with a co-worker over the water cooler. Psychologist Paul Tournier says we have created an image of mankind that is, in essence, a list: physical, emotional, mental and spiritual. Tournier would argue spirituality is not on that list but at the center of the other three. It is the source of our physical, mental and emotional output and the recipient of all input through those means as well. In other words, there is no way to be solely spiritual. Go ahead, be spiritual. Ready?... One...two...three, go! What did you do? Trying to be spiritual away from the rest of our life is like trying to eat without any food or like trying to be a really good driver without ever going down the road. We get in and study the steering wheel and gauges, then we get out of the car and start walking down the road. It is in the living out of our lives that our spirituality can be exercised. Our spiritual battle is fought a million times a day in a million different ways. It is in the effort we put into our work, its in the way we talk to our loved ones, its in the speed with which we return our neighbors borrowed hedge trimmer.

»THE CHRISTIAN GHETTO

Within the Church currently there is a strange effort to counteract this effect by bringing our pseudo-spiritual subculture around with us everywhere we go. We turn the world into a large church service full of people who believe like we do and who don't offend our sensibilities with their sinful behaviors. Opening a phone book, I can find Christian pharmacies, Christian art framing, Christian bakeries and here in my hometown someone has created a business concept out of a cheesy Christian T-shirt. The Lord's Gym Health And Fitness Centers are dedicated to promoting "Fitness for Body & Soul" and offer classes such as Praise Dance, Body of Armor and Chariots of Fire Spin. Now, some might argue such businesses are a good model of stretching the barriers of our spiritual activity beyond Sunday morning. However, all they are doing is adding spiritual language into things that are naturally spiritual because they are part of the human experience God has created. Taking care of your body is spiritual even if you don't play the Newsboys while working on your biceps. These "Christian" shops are doing what all the "secular" shops are doing, but to the exclusion of non-believers. Creating places like this completely removes God's disciples from the world, which doesn't bode well for the world, and I daresay, ends up hurting the Church as well.

What's occurring is the creation of a *ghetto*. The word has long since been associated with inner city housing projects and Elvis's worst song ever, but the ghettos have been around since the middle ages. Then they were walled sections of a city that a religious group (usually Jews) was forced to occupy as a way of keeping them from the rest of the population. Christians appear to be doing it to themselves. And within the walls of this Christian ghetto, we're not only experiencing death in the Church but in the arts as well. Here we are, the group of people that claims to have the corner market on understanding the First and Greatest Artist and we can't even imitate His creative nature as effectively as a world that doesn't know Him.

»THE LAZY CHRISTIAN'S GUIDE TO PRUDENCE

Again, the problem is categories. We have categorized ourselves out of the world. Life is one category. Good music, good art, good health and good prescription drugs are innately spiritual if they are in fact good. We don't need to label something Christian to the exclusion of the rest of the world for it to be good and pure. Because all things that are good and pure are of God, whether the name on it is Rich Mullins or David Gray. All truth is God's truth. If we are seeking God out in everything we do, He will inevitably show up. He doesn't need labels or categories to find us and we shouldn't need them to find Him. Sure, there are experiences you should stay away from, but He has given us a mind, a body of believers and the Holy Spirit to help us decipher what is of Him and what is not. Our categories have become the lazy Christian's guide to prudence. "I don't have to worry about what messages are in this movie, it's Christian." Not only is that argument a dangerous fallacy, but it also leads to the exclusion of truth God is revealing to us through "non-Christian" sources. In God's cosmic video store there is one category: Truth. It's not supposed to be easy. Every experience, every person you meet and every choice you make is a part of the walk. It takes a lot more work and thinking on our part, but we must at least read the back of every video before determining its worth. The good news is there are no late fees. You don't have to have all the answers. We'll have the answers someday, but for now look for God everywhere. And yes, He might even be found in that stupid Elvis song.

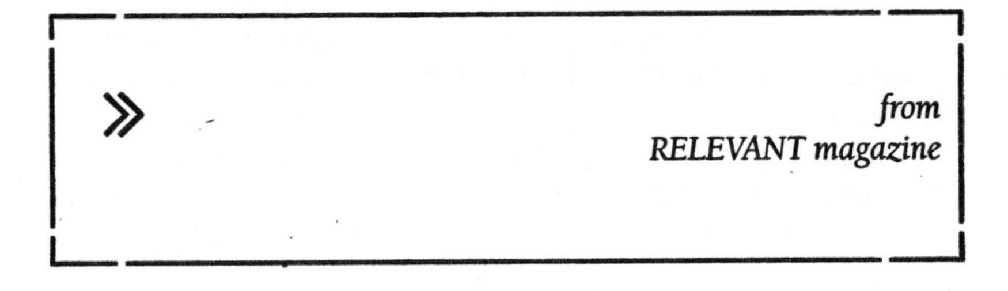

Dan Buck is a drama teacher and freelance writer in Central Florida.

KILLING THE OLD GOD

BY BEN PASLEY

» To choose to worship God is not an entry into a coded textbook of religious activity, nor an affiliation with a system of behaving. It is a mystical step into His presence with both eyes open. If knowing God begins with a real encounter, we should feel free to throw off the old stereotypes we have forced Him to wear. Reaching out to God is a natural and necessary step in the life of someone who feels God reaching out to them. If we can sense His hand extended to us through the world around, then the question is, will we leave it empty, or will we reach out to touch it in return?

One of the most destructive mistakes in the growth of any relationship is to allow assumptions about a person's character to affect the personal discovery process. Sometimes it is a bad first impression that molds a false judgment. Sometimes it is stereotyping that kills the relationship before it can begin. The answer is, of course, to get to know someone personally.

In some cases a pile of misinformation, stereotypes, and bad first impressions has to be worked through before a serious relationship can develop.

"I thought everyone who did that was..."

"He acted like that other guy and so..."

"Before we met I heard that she..."

One of the most popular God-stereotypes for religious people is the "Cosmic Policeman." This is the God who has a whistle in one hand and a large stick in the other. He not only blows the whistle when we do something wrong, he dishes out our punishment with a whack from the happy stick of pain. To make things worse, the whistle, the pointing finger, and the whack are done in broad daylight so that everyone can see. The Cosmic Policeman gets his jollies by humiliating us in public. Occasionally, through the groveling and crying of the "busted," he might show mercy, but it is probably just to induce a much-needed favor. He might even say, "There's going to be hell to pay if I catch you doing that again. I made you. I can make another one just like you!"

He can't really be like this can He? If this were His true nature, what would it say about the meaning of life, the value of creation, the future of our world? How do you see God?

Pope-Meets-Santa Claus?

Distant cloud of nothingness?

Carl Sagan's nemesis?

Omnipotent retiree?

Have you ever wondered where these stereotypes come from? First impressions? Secondhand information? Fairy tales? If we want to move closer to Him, we will have to kill these stereotypes and get to know the *real* Him, not the imagined Him. We will have to demand that He be all that God must really be.

Supernatural.

Endlessly wonderful.

The Lovely.

The Perfect.

The Perfect Lover.

Could He be God and be anything else? Then why settle for less?

Many of us have layers of stereotypes that we force God to wear. Wouldn't it be great if He could come to the party dressed as He really is? We might discover something beautiful behind the hearsay.

»FORGIVING GOD

God has broken many hearts. God has failed many expectations. God has ruined many people's lives. God has ordered the death of many innocents. God has forgotten the homeless. God has unleashed evil on the earth. God is corrupt.

So the story goes.

Do you buy it?

If you do, we are all in a terrible mess. Life has a corrupt beginning, a flawed present, and a hopeless end. This would not be a tragedy we could write about like some dark poet removed from the reality of the drama. There would be no chance to rise above it and gather a rhyming thought; we would be submerged in it.

If you do not buy it, there must be something wrong with our perception. Maybe our perception is *limited*? Just because we cannot understand every move of the Maker we are not entitled to remove Him from the reality of life—even if the reality of life seems flawed and full of inconsistencies and full of evil.

Many philosophers have tried to prove the non-existence of God by using the existence of evil as their proof-text. Without exception they all *have to pretend* to be removed from humanity like an innocent bystander to state their theory of denial. Why? Because the question of *evil in the world* points to the question of evil *in the one making the judgment*. So, if evil exists it has certainly affected our own ability to properly judge God.

Maybe our perception is twisted like an image through warped glass. Small tragedies, little disappointments, and unanswered questions pile one upon the other on the surface of the glass until nothing makes sense anymore. God is out there somewhere, or maybe just on the other side, but we can't make out a clear outline anymore. It is just too hard to understand Him, so forget it.

God needs our forgiveness.

These same kinds of offenses—sometimes intentional, sometimes accidental—often separate lifelong lovers. The romance has a good ending only if they learn these priceless truths along the way:

Sometimes forgiveness is better than understanding.

Sometimes forgiveness is superior to reason.

Sometimes forgiveness is the key to healing the eyes.

God needs to be forgiven.

How has God offended you? How has He let you down? How is God not doing what He should be doing? Or should have done? Tell Him. Do you think He can handle it? Maybe He needs to let us pound His chest and slap His face until things begin to make sense again, or at least until we have exhausted our anger. Most people discover that when they move close enough to see His face, even in the rage of misunderstanding, that there is something to learn. They discover the unexpected God. Stereotypes began to melt from the heat of His compassion and the washing of His tears. How He reacts to human pain makes a difference.

If we don't forgive Him for what He has done or what He has not done, we will always be trapped in our bitterness and we may never know Him. We must find a way to forgive if we are going to know Him better. Maybe as we move in closer and choose to speak the truth, whether pleasant or harsh, we will find that honesty is the key to any good relationship, even a relationship with God.

»FINDING THE BEAUTIFUL

More than one relationship has been saved from impending doom (or at least terrible mediocrity) by the wonderful gift of the unexpected compliment. However silly that may sound, the *unexpected compliment* goes a long, long way. Praise is a healer of wounds. A gesture of adoration in a moment when it is not looked for can make a person's day. Doesn't everyone love a rich compliment? We are not talking about the patronizing stuff designed to manipulate a situation—we are talking about real adoration.

One sure way to build a bridge into the presence of God is to practice the art of the spontaneous compliment. Even the most difficult person has at least one admirable quality to compliment.

God has an infinite number of wonderful things to adore. Finding them can become a lifelong sport.

The simplest way to build the bridge to God through compliments is to recognize the things He has done well. It is the same in any relationship. When we first get to know someone we can't speak our appreciation for the deep things in their life, so we begin by commenting on the things they obviously do well:

"You are a good listener. I really appreciate it."

"You are really in shape. Do you work out?"

"It's been a long time since I met a person who is so organized!"

Little things count. People who want to touch a real God might need to start with a patient understanding of the relationship's progress. Start small. Go carefully. Ask questions. Expect answers. Compliment. Offer thanks for little things. The person who looks for the positive things in the life of a new friend will usually find them.

Admiring someone can open the door to a new part of his or her life. Often they let their guard down in the face of appreciation and praise.

They let us in a little further.

What follows is a Path of Seven for rediscovering God. These exercises can help clear the path of old stereotypes into the true nature of God. In these we can remove the bitterness of unforgiveness. They can also help wash the face of God so we can see Him better. Don't be in a hurry to complete them all at once.

1. In a quiet place write down this question: Why would an artist count any brush stroke as a waste of time? Underneath it write: How could the God who created every thing not care deeply for everything He created? Write a short answer for each. Does the answer say anything about how He must feel about you?

2. Find a high place. As you look out over the horizon consider the vastness of God. Pick up a rock and hold it in one hand. Consider the way God has often been small

enough to fit in your pocket when you needed Him. Ask God why He doesn't react harshly when we treat Him like an optional thing.

3. Take out a piece of paper. Describe how God has offended you, or let you down, or failed to come through. Find a quiet place and ask God to show you where He was and what He was doing during the offenses. Write down what you sense Him saying.

4. Draw a picture of God. What does He look like? Does He wear a robe? Why? Is He threatening? Why? What is around Him? Why? Has God communicated any of these characteristics to you through a trustworthy agent? If not, where did you learn them?

5. Walk in a garden and ask yourself aloud: How could God possibly love only religious people? Does God love everyone or only some? Why? If He loves us all the same, then what happens to His heart if some love Him in return and others do not?

6. While driving alone in your car, say out loud, "God, I refuse to believe the slander about You without testing it for myself. I also refuse to believe that You do not exist because I have been raised a skeptic. God, I want You to reveal Yourself to me personally, and until You do so I realize that I have no right to pre-judge You with partial history or secondhand theory."

7. Walk through a mall. People make a lot of stuff, don't they? Think of the things God has made that really impress you. Spend some time telling God how great you think some of His creations are. Try to go on and on about the miracle of their existence and beauty.

»

from
Enter the Worship Circle

Ben Pasley is a songwriter and producer.
He and his wife Robin form the music group
100 Portraits, which he founded in 1993.

The Alarm Clock Moment

By Ben Pasley

In our world we no longer admire teachers as much as we admire helpers. Teachers, in our mind, come with a prepackaged lesson plan and give lectures that we should write down. Helpers, on the other hand, come to us with personal concern and a belief that we have inside of us the tools to excel, but we simply need encouragement and maybe a working model to follow. For the academic mind this rings of "inductive versus deductive" theories of learning—the difference between discovering through experience and flatly assuming the points of a lecture. Being "taught" implies that we don't already know something, but being "helped" supports our position that we have all we need—we simply need a little encouragement to help us find it.

This short journey into the Worship Circle may offer some help in reaching our ultimate destination. Just what is that destination? We know that it is not found in the material world. "Things" do not contain the kind of treasure that we seek. We all seem to be searching for something genuinely trustworthy in life, and we all have a sense that this search has something to do with the mystery of eternity and the world beyond. This common pursuit leads us to the common need for a *helper*—someone or something that can challenge us to discover Truth. No one has to teach us that we should hunger for the supernatural; the hunger is already in us—and we know it.

No one can hand it to us.

My suspicion is that we all have a capacity to become great, to do well, and to move to the next level of living, but we often miss our opportunity to "wake up" to the best kind of motivation. Many people stay up late waiting for the "late-night-infomercial-you-didn't-know-you-needed-this-did-you?" kind of motivation that dissipates after coffee the next morning. This kind of motivation is external and temporary. The motivation that we need to excel must come from deep within.

Humanity possesses a myriad of these deep, internal motivations: some physical, some mental, and some supernatural. To deny any one of these motivators' proper exercise is to deny one's own human essence. Humans are driven to use their physical capacities to move, communicate, and express themselves. Humans must exercise the ability to think, dream, and engage the world with their minds. And, without a doubt, humans are obsessed with discovering a meaningful interaction with the world beyond its fingertips in order to exercise the spiritual part of life.

The question for us is: Have we given proper exercise to each of these areas?

In the physical realm we are constantly coached and challenged to work our way into better condition. Be thinner, taller, tighter, and sexier! Fitness and physical beauty is a mega-million dollar industry. The free-market is well aware that we are easily motivated to improve our body and "look." The challenge to improve ourselves physically might often come from *without*, but it gains momentum when fueled by the ready passion from *within*. No one has to teach us to celebrate the winner of the decathlon or to admire the beauty of the human form. The real challenge is not in deciding to improve physically, but the decision *how* it will be done.

Concerning the mental realm, it might be fun to pick on the "brain" of the class in the sixth grade, but by the time we graduate from college we see things in a different light. That same "brain" is now driving the car we want and making the money we wish we had. The passage of time proves that being smart...is smart. Movies, books, and history are filled with the stories of the thinkers, writers, and solution people who changed the world.

Communities spend millions of dollars on education and mental training to advance the thinking part of the individual because it will boost the subsequent wealth of the community. In this new global economy we all strive to think smarter, read faster, outwit our adversary, and recover quickly from the personal computer crash. It is now a brain-sport world, and we are all searching for the path to excellence.

Throughout history the supernatural part of man has been just as challenged as the physical and mental parts, because it is just as real and ready for inspiration. Recently, however, we have entered a new era of intense spiritual pursuit. Something has happened in our world community that has shifted us into mystical overdrive. Now our challenge is not *whether we will* exercise our internal drive to reach out to the supernatural, it is *how we will reach out.* The new confusion is that in our modern world of computers, television, and cars we have access to all the external voices—and they are all competing for supremacy. We are challenged to get in touch with our spirit guides via 900 numbers, we can find our cosmic center through the huge New Age section at the bookstore, and we can watch The *X-Files* almost any day of the week. We can get *Touched by an Angel*, or freak watching *The Blair Witch Project*, or entertain ourselves with any number of apocalyptic myths that the new millennium has ushered in. For a more heady approach we are pressed to read Hume, Nietzsche, C.S. Lewis, and Asimov for religious or irreligious views on religion. In-a-“pinch” prayer is always good—even for the atheist—and many of us are experimenting with churches and religious gatherings with either ourselves or our children in mind. We have come to grips with the fact that we have supernatural urges—deep internal motivation—but where do we go from here? How do we properly exercise this desire?

No one can hand it to us.

While some might try to capitalize on this spiritual awakening in pursuit of our bank accounts, there must be some who are willing to give us a compass, an encouragement, and a gesture toward the horizon without ulterior motive. There must be some "helpers" out there who want to see the look on our collective face as we discover for ourselves what is real and exciting about the supernatural world. We are all on a spiritual mountain climb.

To enter the Worship Circle is to enter the world of the supernatural with a freedom to experiment, to discover its treasures, and to find its center—the goal of our mystical pursuit. Worship, itself, will help us embrace the surest part of the world beyond and mature in our experience with it. Worship will exercise our supernatural life. Without exercise this spiritual life would atrophy and fade away leaving us less whole, less alive, and less human. This adventure into the Worship Circle can help us to not only "wake up" what may have fallen asleep, but also to make decisions about our spiritual path among all the competing voices.

No one can hand it to us.

Will we reach out to find it?

» *from*
Enter the Worship Circle

Ben Pasley is a songwriter and producer.
He and his wife Robin form the music group
100 Portraits, which he founded in 1993.

Growing Through the Whispers and Silence

By Margaret Feinberg

WHY IS GOD SOMETIMES SILENT?

One of the great benefits of God's silence is it makes you appreciate the times He speaks. God's silence teaches that when the faucet of God's revelation is running, when you can feel His sweet presence and comprehend His sweet words, get all you can get. Drink in all of His revelations and truth you possibly can. Never neglect or ignore His warm invitation to spend time with you. It is precious. And you never know. He may be pouring out on you because a wilderness period is around the next corner. God reserves the right to be silent. He reserves the right to delay answers, leave certain issues unaddressed, and become seemingly quiet.

WHY? THERE ARE A MYRIAD OF REASONS

You may have asked the wrong question. You may have asked to know something that God is not ready to reveal or something that could be detrimental to you or someone else if it was revealed.

For example, you meet someone you don't really like. You begin asking God why you aren't getting along with the person and what is wrong with the person. All the while, God wants you to focus on the strengths of the individual.

Or you may have an issue in which you jump ahead in your request. You may have placed your house on the market and asked God, "When will you bring a buyer?" But you never bothered to ask Him if you should sell your home in the first place.

You may be out of God's timing. There is a story about James Garfield, who before he became President of the United States, served as the principal of Hiram College in Ohio. A father of one of the students asked him whether a course could be simplified so his son could go through more quickly.

Garfield replied, "Certainly, but it all depends on what you want to make of your boy. When God wants to make an oak tree, he takes a hundred years. When he wants to make a squash, he requires only two summers."[1]

Remember, God works on a different timetable. Sometimes the issues that are the most pressing on your heart are not the most pressing on His. He has an order and timing for everything. Ecclesiastes 3:1 reminds us, "There is a time for everything, and a season for every activity under heaven."

ARE YOU WILLING TO WAIT FOR THE ANSWER?

You may not be at a place where you can handle the answer. God may choose not to answer you, because you are not strong enough to handle it.

Corrie ten Boom's father illustrated this truth beautifully when at a young age Corrie asked him a question about sex. Recognizing his daughter's naiveté, his response was laden with wisdom.

> He turned to look at me, as he always did when answering a question, but to my surprise he said nothing. At last he stood up, lifted his traveling case from the rack over our heads, and set it on the floor.
>
> "Will you carry it off the train, Corrie?" he said.
>
> I stood up and tugged at it. It was crammed with the watches and spare parts he had purchased that morning.
>
> "It's too heavy," I said.
>
> "Yes," he said. "And it would be a pretty poor father who would ask his little girl to carry such a load. It's the same way, Corrie, with knowledge. Some knowledge is too heavy for children. When you are older and stronger you can bear it. For now you must trust me to carry it for you."
>
> And I was satisfied. More than satisfied-wonderfully at peace. There were answers to this and all my hard questions-for now I was content to leave them in my father's keeping."[2]

This same theme was explored in the award-winning film *Life Is Beautiful.* The movie follows the adventure of a zesty, comical fellow named Guido who falls head over heels (literally) for a young schoolteacher. Their love blossoms into marriage, and they enjoy life with their young son.

Halfway through the film, the family is ripped away from their home and sent to a Nazi concentration camp where Guido does everything he can to hide the horrors of the war from his young son. In this tender, noble story, hiding the boy from the terrible reality of the camp is an act of love, courage, and sacrifice.

This theme is biblical. Jesus once told His disciples, "I have much more to say to you, more than you can now bear" (JOHN 16:12). When Christ was questioned about the act of washing his disciples' feet, he responded, "Now that you know these things, you will be blessed if you do them" (JOHN 13:17). God knows our limitations even better than we do.

You may be asking about something that is none of your business. God is all knowing, but humans are not. They were never intended to be. Sometimes you will be asking for information or insight into something that could easily be a distraction or could harden your heart toward a situation or person.

Sometimes God withholds something from you because it can harm you. Remember the tree of the knowledge of good and evil in the Garden of Eden. Genesis 2:17 records God's command, "But you must not eat from the tree of the knowledge of good and evil, for when you eat of it you will surely die."

There is knowledge that God holds back from us for our own good. There may be someone else involved in a situation or group who is supposed to seek the Lord on a particular issue. He is waiting for that person to step up to the plate, not you.

You may be living with sin or compromise in your life that blocks your ability to hear from God. If you are living with your boyfriend, God may not be willing to tell you whether or not the person is "the one." If you're cheating on your income taxes, God may not respond to your request for wisdom as to where to invest money.

You may not be in a position to hear an answer. When God is silent, reflect on why He is silent. Do you have sin or compromise in your life? Sin blocks us from God. It's not that God turns His back on us, but that we turn our backs on Him.

Disobedience can be sin. If you have not been obedient to the last thing God asked you to do, why would He entrust you with more? God will often wait for you to be obedient on small things before He will entrust you with larger ones.

Silence is not always a sin issue. You need to reflect on what God may be trying to teach you. Is this a season of growth or testing? Have you been spending enough time with Him to hear from Him?

Circumstances—both physical and spiritual—may delay God's answer. Daniel, the famed lion's den survivor, had to wait three weeks before God answered his request because of spiritual warfare.

Daniel 10:12-14 records, "'Do not be afraid, Daniel. Since the first day that you set your mind to gain understanding and to humble yourself before your God, your words were heard, and I have come in response to them. But the prince of the Persian kingdom resisted me twenty-one days. Then Michael, one of the chief princes, came to help me, because I was detained there with the king of Persia. Now I have come to explain to you what will happen to your people in the future, for the vision concerns a time yet to come.'"

Daniel was not the only one who had to wait for God to speak. When Moses went up on Mount Sinai, the glory of the Lord settled on the mountain. According to Exodus 24:16, "For six days the cloud covered the mountain, and on the seventh day the LORD called to Moses from within the cloud."

Scripture records that Jeremiah also had to wait for the word of the Lord (JEREMIAH 42:7). Following Christ's ascension, those in the upper room waited forty days before God poured out His spirit upon them and used them to speak in tongues and declare the mighty deeds of God (ACTS 2:11).

God may be withholding an answer because He has something He wants to work out in an individual or group of people's lives that takes time. There may be things God is trying to teach someone about Himself that requires Him to wait to answer our request because of the people involved.

After being entrusted with great insight into the future, Daniel was told, "Go your way, Daniel, because the words are closed up and sealed until the time of the end" (DANIEL 12:9).

God may be trying to increase your patience, diligence, or faith. Why is God silent? One of the biggest reasons is to grow our faith. If you have ever seen the picture that accompanies the famous "Footprints" poem, you'll notice there is only one set of footprints in the sand. Those are moments Jesus is carrying you.

But there are also times in the Christian walk when two sets of footprints are spaced further apart. You can walk this part of the journey without being carried. You don't need your hand held. You know the path. You are still in His presence. You are still connected, but at times God will take a step back to grow our faith. Jeremiah 29:12-13 promises, "Then you will call upon me and come and pray to me, and I will listen to you. You will seek me and find me when you seek me with all your heart."

Waiting for God to answer naturally stretches you and demands more patience and perseverance than you may have originally been willing to offer. God is forever loving you and wanting to grow you into the image of His Son. Hebrews 11:6 promises, "Anyone who comes to him must believe that he exists and that he rewards those who earnestly seek him."

In *Disappointment With God*, Philip Yancey observes that we, as humans, have little understanding of what our faith means to God. He writes:

> In some mysterious way, Job's terrible ordeal was "worth" it to God because it went to the core of the entire human experiment. More than Job's faith, the motive behind all creation was at stake. Ever since God took the "risk" of making room for free human beings, faith—true, unbribed, freely offered faith—has had an intrinsic value to God we can barely imagine. There is no better way for us to express love to God than by exercising fidelity to him.[3]

At times, tests of faith can seem like tough love. No matter how difficult life may become, He doesn't want you to give up. He is after your best. He wants to answer your prayer. Keep seeking. Keep knocking, and whatever you do, don't give up too soon.

The bottom line is that while God knows everything, He does not reveal everything even when you ask Him. In Acts 20:22, Paul says, "And now, compelled by the Spirit, I am going to Jerusalem, not knowing what will happen to me there."

In the face of such silence and uncertainty, Paul had grown to a point were His faith did not waiver. He didn't have to know what was going on. He just had to know God. He goes on to write, "I only know that in every city the Holy Spirit warns me that prison and hardships are facing me. However, I consider my life worth nothing to me, if only I may finish the race and complete the task the Lord Jesus has given me—the task of testifying to the gospel of God's grace" (ACTS 20:23-24).

Paul wasn't focused on the details of his mission or what was waiting for him during each visit. The Lord had whispered that prison and difficulties were coming. He didn't know the form of the imprisonment, but girded with the limited knowledge, he didn't lose heart or hope. He was focused on God.[4]

WHAT IF I HAVEN'T HEARD FROM GOD?

You've prayed. You've asked. You've pleaded. You've begged. You've done everything you know to do. You're out of time. The mortgage is due. The car is about to be repossessed. The graduation ceremony is over. The deadlines are upon you. And still, God is silent. What do you do?

It's a fair question. And, there are a small handful of responses. First, never give up. Study and know the promises of God. Are there any promises or whispers He gave you before the recent silence? Cling to those.

Second, don't be surprised if God moves in the final hour. God likes to stretch and strengthen our faith. To do so, He will often wait until the last hour to move on our behalf.

Third, take a step back from the situation and try to remember any times God may have been trying to speak to you. Often, during stressful or trying times, God is speaking. We are simply not listening. Take some time to reflect on the recent past. Has there been any godly counsel, Scripture, or circumstantial leading? Did God speak, and you just missed it?

There are times when God will be silent, and you will be forced to make a decision. Life circumstances dictate something must be done. Maybe your lease is up, and if you don't move out then you'll be fined or even arrested. Maybe your mortgage is due, and the bank won't take "no" for an answer. Maybe the event is tomorrow, and the last flight there leaves in an hour. You are forced to act one way or the other.

If you find yourself pinned in a corner by circumstance, remember God has not left you. He is still with you, and He still desires the best for you. He may not have ordered a skywriting plane for you, but He still wants to lead you.

On a practical level, reflect on your options in light of the questions:

- Does the option line up with Scripture?
- Does the option line up with circumstance?
- Does the option line up with the wise counsel?
- Does the option line up with my vision and goals?
- Does the option leave me with a sense of peace?

- Is this an option I would naturally think of on my own?
- Is the option blanketed in love?

When you have an option or answer that aligns with these questions, then step out. It may be one of those stumbling moments, or it may be a tremendous moment of faith and spiritual growth.

WHY DOES GOD SAY "NO"?

As you seek God's will on various aspects of life, you will eventually hear God say, "No." It may be to an opportunity, relationship, job, or ministry. It may be to any of a thousand different things you ask Him. It may be something you really want. It can be hard to hear "no."

Sometimes God says "no" to let you out of a situation. Elisabeth Elliot observes:

> "Sometimes our prayers for deliverance from conditions which are morally indispensable—that is, conditions which are absolutely necessary to our redemption. God does not grant us those requests. He will not because He loves us with a pure and implacable purpose: that Christ be formed in us."[5]

"No" can be a hard answer to hear, but it isn't the only one. Over the course of a lifetime, God will say many things that aren't easy to hear. He isn't in the ear-tickling business.

Remember the story of the rich ruler's encounter with Christ. The young man's well-polished, well-fed appearance must have stood in stark contrast to Jesus' travel-worn presentation. Yet Jesus didn't soften his reply for the young man: "...You still lack one thing. Sell everything you have and give to the poor, and you will have treasure in heaven. Then come, follow me" (LUKE 18:22).

Sometimes God will speak hard words to you and then give you a choice: obey or disobey. The temptation is always to do the latter, but the rewards are promised to those who do the former.

Over the last few years, I have asked the Lord for guidance and wisdom on whether to pursue multiple opportunities and repeatedly heard, "No." Only recently have some of the things that He had said "No" to begun to play out and I have been able to see what would have happened if I had disobeyed. In every situation, I thank God for saving me from the heartache, pain, and disappointment that would have followed.

"No" can be one of God's kindest replies. He knows what is best for us, and when we are reaching for bronze, He reminds us gold is available if we will just wait on Him.

HOW DO I AVOID LOOKING LIKE A FLAKE?

If you aren't already asking yourself this question, you should be. You have heard the phrases, "God told me..." or "God is going to..." And, it does not happen. The claim doesn't pan out. You are left with one of two conclusions: either the person was off base or God didn't come through. And it's probably not the latter.

The result is a long list of abuses and unnecessary pain in the body of Christ. Rather than add to the list of abuses of hearing from God, I encourage you to follow the practice of Mary. God whispered to Jesus' mother many times about her special Son. Scripture records that Mary was overshadowed by the Most High. The angel Gabriel made a personal visit. She witnessed the miracles surrounding her relative Elizabeth when she became pregnant and gave birth to John the Baptist. When her Son was finally born, wise men delivered gifts and strangers visited their humble stable. In the face of so much God activity and numerous whispers, Luke 2:19 reveals Mary did something very wise: she "treasured up all these things and pondered them in her heart."

She knew that God whispers are really treasures, and they need to be treated as such. Whenever God whispers something to you, hold it in high regard. Keep it near your heart. Let it roll over in your mind and spirit. Recognize the words He is speaking to you are sacred and often meant just for you.

Never forget that God has secrets. He is an all-knowing, all-encompassing God, and He has things He simply chooses not to share with everyone. First Corinthians 2:7 says, "No, we speak of God's secret wisdom, a wisdom that has been hidden and that God destined for our glory before time began." Daniel 2:22 describes God as one who "reveals deep and hidden things; he knows what lies in darkness, and light dwells with him."

Christ revealed some of God's secrets and fulfilled what was spoken through the prophets as one who "will open my mouth in parables" and "utter things hidden since the creation of the world" (MATTHEW 13:35). Paul reflected on this hidden wisdom as "...God's secret wisdom, a wisdom that has been hidden and that God destined for our glory before time began" (1 CORINTHIANS 2:7).

God is not a motor mouth; many times it is important for you to keep things between yourselves.

WHEN CAN I SHARE THE WHISPER WITH SOMEONE ELSE?

There are times, however, when it's appropriate to share. For example, when a whisper involves a large group of people or something God is going to do within a community. But before you share, I would encourage you to ask yourself the following as safeguards:

- Am I open to correction if I'm wrong?
- Is there anyone I need to get permission from to share this whisper? (pastor, leader etc.)
- Am I willing to be silent if the authority over me asks me to not deliver the message?
- Could anyone be hurt by sharing this whisper?
- Will I be made to look like a fool if it isn't fulfilled?
- Will another person be embarrassed if this isn't fulfilled?
- Will God be embarrassed if this isn't fulfilled?
- Will my word be less credible if this isn't fulfilled?

If you feel led to share what you've heard from God, then be wise with your words. At all costs, avoid using phrases such as, "Thus saith the Lord," "God told me," and "God said." To most people, these phrases suggest you heard audibly and with 100 percent precision. Which, if you didn't, will be misleading. It will also conjure up most people's memories of encounters with false prophets and overly zealous church members.

The "Thus-saith-the-Lord" approach also makes people not want to confront or correct you. When you use that particular phrase, most people are uncomfortable with challenging the message, even though it may really need to be questioned. Some believers have a difficult time with prophetic words and taking this approach may make it harder for them to receive the message.

Temper your words instead. Use phrases such as, "I was praying, and I think God was showing me...," "I feel like God was impressing on my heart..." or "I can't explain it, but I just have this sense that..."

On the surface, using qualifiers may seem to weaken the message, but if God is in the message, then it will grip people's hearts no matter what phrase you use. Using such phrases will also give God more time to work.

There are times when others can learn from the whispers you've heard—whether it's a word of correction or revelation. Be sensitive to the Holy Spirit's leading as to when to share those words.

If you're an eager beaver to tell everyone every single thing you hear from the Lord, then it's probably time to reflect on some of the Old Testament passages that mention what happens to false or disobedient prophets. It will give you a healthy fear of God.

SOURCES

1 Garfield, Morgan, *Robert J. Nelson's Complete Book of Stories, Illustrations & Quotes*. (Nashville: Thomas Nelson, 2000), p. 601.

2 Ten Boom, Corrie. *The Hiding Place*. (Grand Rapids: Chosen, 1996), p. 30-31. Used with permission.

3 Yancey, Philip. *Disappointment With God.* (Grand Rapids: Zondervan, 1988), p. 209. Taken from *Disappointment With God.* Copyright 1988 by Zondervan Publishing House. Used by permission of Zondervan.

4 "Many Reasons Why God Delays Answers" from Joy Dawson's *Forever Ruined For the Ordinary* (Nashville: Thomas Nelson), pp. 90-110 was helpful in writing this section on God's silence.

5 Elliot, Elisabeth. *A Lamp For My Feet.* (Ann Arbor: Vine Books, 1985), p. 131. *From A Lamp For My Feet* by Elisabeth Elliot. 1985 by Elisabeth Elliot. Published by Servant Publications, P.O. Box 8617, Ann Arbor, Michigan, 48107. Used with permission.

» *from*
God Whispers

Margaret Feinberg is a writer based in Steamboat Springs, Colorado. She has written for a variety of nationally recognized magazines and is a contributing writer to *Enjoying God* and *I AM RELEVANT.*

The Invitation of the Voice

By Margaret Feinberg

» When a friend calls you, how do you know it's your friend and not just a prank caller? How do you know it's your friend and not your mother, father, brother, boss, or neighbor?

You know because you know your friend. By spending time with your friend, you know the average speed of the person's words. You know the inflections. You recognize the tones. You know the voice. That is the way it should be with God.

You know Him—His character, His nature, His word, His interests, His pleasures and displeasure, His joys and hurts—so well that you recognize Him and His involvement in your life.

If you don't recognize someone's voice, it may mean you haven't been listening. If you don't recognize someone's voice, it may mean you haven't been spending enough time with the person. If you don't recognize someone's voice, it may mean you need to get to know the person better.

God is inviting you to know more than just His voice; He is inviting you to know Him. It's an awesome opportunity. Elijah is a man who accepted the invitation. Even at his lowest moments, he could still discern the word of the Lord. First Kings 19 describes the famed prophet tucked away in a cave.

"What are you doing here?" the Lord asked.

Exhausted and disgruntled, Elijah explained, "I have been zealous for you, but everyone else has rejected your promises, broken down your altars and killed the other prophets. Now I'm the only one left, and they're going to kill me, too."

Elijah was ready to call it quits, but the Lord didn't immediately answer the prophet's concerns. Instead, He asked the prophet to do something a little odd: go out and stand on the mountain and wait. God was going to pass by.

Elijah obeyed. Waiting in one of the mountain's many caves, Elijah could hear the breeze beginning to pick up. Before he could tuck himself any further in the cave, a thunderous wind hit the mountainside, shattering rocks in all its fierceness. But the Lord was not in the wind. A few moments later Elijah could feel the ground tremble; he began to lose his footing. A violent earthquake shook everything that seemed unshakable. But the Lord was not in the earthquake. Then a sudden blaze of heat, an actual fire, came down from heaven. But the Lord was not in the fire. Elijah's heart was filled with fear. What would be next? A lightning bolt? A flood? A volcanic outburst?

Elijah waited. In the still silence, Elijah could hear a gentle whisper. He knew it was the Lord. He got up and "pulled his cloak over his face and went out and stood at the mouth of the cave" (1 KINGS 19:13).

The quiet voice asked Elijah the same question it had before: "What are you doing here?" To which Elijah gave the same reply. Then, the Lord answered Him with specific instructions and encouraged him that he was not the only one—there were 7,000 others who had not bowed their knee to Baal.

God pulled the unexpected on Elijah. Rather than give an answer, God gave Himself. Rather than manifest Himself in all His brilliant glory and splendid power, He chose to use a whisper.

God doesn't always whisper. Sometimes He shouts and creates quite a clamor. When God visited Moses and the multitudes at Mt. Sinai, he didn't use His "inside voice."

Exodus 19:16-20 describes: "On the morning of the third day there was thunder and lightning, with a thick cloud over the mountain, and a very loud trumpet blast. Everyone in the camp trembled. Then Moses led the people out of the camp to meet with God, and they stood at the foot of the mountain. Mount Sinai was covered with smoke, because the LORD descended on it in fire. The smoke billowed up from it like smoke from a furnace, the whole mountain trembled violently, and the sound of the trumpet grew louder and louder. Then Moses spoke and the voice of God answered him."

Both Moses and Elijah knew God well enough to recognize Him in the midst of a cacophony of action and noise. They knew God well enough to recognize Him, not just the signs of Him.

This book could have been titled *God Thunders* or *God Quakes* and still have been taken from the Scripture. It is titled *God Whispers* because the real focus isn't as much about how God speaks as it is about the posture of our relationship with Him.

To hear someone's whisper, you need to be near him or her. Whispering doesn't work very well if the person you are speaking to is on the other side of the room. God isn't content with a long-distance relationship; He wants an intimate one. The posture of this type of relationship is found in John 13:23: "There was reclining on Jesus' breast one of His disciples, whom Jesus loved" (NAS).

It's an intimate portrait. John, believed to be the one described in this verse, is nestled against the Messiah's chest—an expression of reliance and vulnerability. It feels warm and safe. As John turns his head, he can hear the steady heartbeat of his teacher, savior, and friend. It probably wasn't the first time this disciple—who had built a special relationship with Jesus—felt the Master's warm embrace, but unlike previous times, this was a precarious moment in history: the evening of Jesus' betrayal.

Jesus announces that the betrayer is at the table. The disciples perform a quick audit of each other and their own hearts. Breaking the silence, the rock of the group, Simon Peter, looks around the table and gestures to John, "Tell us who it is of whom He is speaking" (v. 24, NAS). The request seems uncharacteristic for the outspoken disciple. Simon Peter is anything but a shy guy. He never had a problem speaking up before, but now his tongue is tied. It's a simple question, but Simon Peter defers it to the one closest to Christ.

"Lord, who is it?" the disciple asks. Jesus exposes Judas.

On the eve of the announcement of Jesus' betrayal, anyone could have been leaning against Jesus' breast. During the previous three years of ministry, multitudes followed Him. In a commissioning, He sent out seventy-two to do the work of the Father. He called twelve to be His disciples. Three were permitted to visit the Mount where Jesus was transfigured. But on that fateful night, only one was leaning against His breast.

What are you leaning against? I believe that the position of being poised against Jesus' breast is available to every believer.

British preacher Alexander Maclaren once observed, "We are able to have as much of God as we want. Christ puts the key to His treasure chest in our hands and invites us to take all we desire. If someone is allowed into a bank vault, told to help himself to the money, and leaves without one cent, whose fault is it if he remains poor? And whose fault is it that Christians usually have some meager portions of the free riches of God?"[1]

How much of God do you really want?

THE URGENCY OF THE INVITATION

Jesus says, "Here I am! I stand at the door and knock. If anyone hears my voice and opens the door, I will come in and eat with him, and he with me" (REVELATION 3:20). This verse isn't just an invitation to become a believer; it's an invitation to live as one.

Notice that Jesus comes to the door empty-handed. He doesn't say, "Open the door and I'll give you a signed and sealed salvation card or a basket full of blessings." In fact, He doesn't bring anything: just Himself. And a small promise to dine together.

Jesus isn't knocking to see what He can give or what He can get. He is knocking because He wants to share a relationship. That is His focus.

I believe we live in an hour when Jesus' knock is becoming more urgent. Like John on the night of Jesus' betrayal, we are living in precarious times. It's not just nice, but necessary to have a deep, intimate relationship with God.

Doug Metzger, author of *Liberty Through The Cross*, describes a vision he had of how the Church was formed in America. God gave him the image of rain falling upon a range of mountains. As the rain fell, it drained down the path of least resistance, ending at the base of the mountains in a desert. The water collected at the desert floor until it developed into a vast lake. Standing at the shore, you could see nothing but water in every direction. As soon as the sun came up, the lake dried up because it didn't have any depth.

The Lord spoke to Metzger's heart and said, *"This is the Church in America. It was formed through following the path of least resistance. It is vast. It is huge. But as soon as there is some heat, it will dry up. Except for a few pools that have a little bit of depth."*[2]

How do you have depth? How do you anchor yourself in the knowledge of God so that no matter what happens—whether the winds of prosperity or adversity blow over—you remain in Him? The answer is simple: by knowing Him.

Living out that answer will cost you everything. It will require sacrifice, dying to self, and choosing the things of God over the things of this world.

Wherever you are and whatever you are doing, God wants to take you one step further. If you have a strong relationship with Him, He wants to make it stronger. If you have discovered deep things of God, He wants to take you deeper. If you are living a holy life, He wants to make you more holy.

Whenever God thinks of you, He has your best in mind. He has plans to take you further, deeper, and higher than you have ever dreamed, but it is hard to get there if you are not listening. It's going to be tough to go anywhere significant if you are more plugged into the television than you are to God. It's going to be hard to complete the journey if you're spending more of your time at the mall than listening to His message. It's going to be nearly impossible to receive His best if you're working more than you're willing to obey.

How do you deepen your relationship with God? By seeking God and looking for ways to spend more time with Him. Who are the people in your life that you have the deepest relationships with? Those who you have spent the most time with. If you reflect on those relationships, you will recognize there were many opportunities when you had to pick up the phone, write the letter, or send the email to contact them.

Though the devices are different, building a relationship with God is the same. You have to turn off the television, open your Bible, get down on your knees, and seek Him. You can't continue your life the way it is and still grow to your full potential in God.

Insanity has been defined as "doing the same things and expecting different results." Spiritual insanity is living the same life and expecting different results. If you want more of God, then you are going to have to change your schedule and priorities.

In a prayer for mercy and help, the prophet Isaiah laments that there is no one "who arouses himself to take hold of Thee" (ISAIAH 64:7, NAS).

Where do you begin? Try doubling the amount of time you spend with Him each day. Try doubling the amount of time you spend reading the Bible. Try doubling any of your spiritual disciplines as well as exploring different ones. Memorize Scripture. Journal. Evangelize. Find a mentor. Mentor others.

How do you get to know God? The same way you would a friend. Think about it. You would call the person. You would invite the person over to share a meal. You would listen. You would share. You would look for ways to serve. You would find out what the person likes or dislikes. You would take trips together. Look for every opportunity to know God.

Consider your daily schedule. What does it include? A workout at the gym? A trip to the post office? A lunch hour? A commute? Look for ways to include God in your activities. Invite Him to accompany you by talking to Him. Look for moments—even if it's only ten or twenty seconds—to steal away with Him. It will require effort, but it is possible to reshape your inner life so it is focused around Him. As you seek Him, you will find yourself abiding in Him.

Jesus' invitation isn't only to know God but to abide in Him. John 15:4-5 says, "Remain in Me, and I will remain in you. No branch can bear fruit by itself, it must remain in the vine. Neither can you bear fruit unless you remain in me. I am the vine; you are the branches. If a man remains in me and I in him, he will bear much fruit; apart from me you can do nothing."

Jesus' command to abide in Him is actually an invitation to live in the presence of God. It is a place of rest and quiet confidence where God is in charge.

In *Liberty Through The Cross*, Doug Metzer writes, "What is abiding? It literally means 'to continue to be present' or 'to be held or kept continually.' It is a posture of being poised towards God. It is being able to discern God's voice and knowing how to act upon what He speaks to your heart. It is knowing God as He is. Abiding is embracing and living in the access to the Father that Jesus purchased with His blood."[3]

Abiding implies dependence. Metzer colorfully explains that abiding is "standing in God, though all hell comes against us, knowing He is the author and finisher of our faith. Abiding is not doing. Abiding is being."[4]

When Jesus spent time with His disciples, He provided a portrait of abiding. He ate meals with them. He traveled with them. He talked, laughed, and shared with them. Before Jesus expressed the importance of abiding in John 15, He lived it with them. John 14:25 says, "These things I have spoken to you, while abiding with you" (NAS).

A Bible professor once told his class that in the morning during his prayer time he had asked the Holy Spirit to stay with Him that day. He asked the Holy Spirit not to leave Him. He heard the Holy Spirit respond, "You don't leave me."

That should become the goal of our lives—to walk with Him daily. Though I still stumble, I have discovered that listening and obeying God is one of the richest and most rewarding aspects of life. Like the Israelites in the desert, I have found God's whispers to be like manna—something I need every day.

The Israelites didn't wake up in their tents with full stomachs every morning, they had to go out and gather the precious, life-giving bread. In the same way, I need to gather God's Word and wisdom for my life every day.

When I don't take time to be with God and hear Him, I start to lose my way. I lose sight of His promises, what He intends for me, and what He thinks of me. I begin focusing on the world and listening to its messages instead. It usually isn't long before I find myself starving spiritually for God. Now that I've tasted of His treasures and His kingdom, the world just doesn't satisfy. I want more of Him.

Why? Because He is beyond amazing. Some of the whispers I've heard over the years have transformed the way I live and interact with the world. I remember several years ago sitting in the front row of small church in a suburb of Tegucigalpa, Honduras. Even after developing survival-like Spanish skills during my stint in Spain, I still couldn't understand the lyrics during worship, but I could sense God's presence.

I stood with my eyes closed worshipping God when I began to see a picture of the wonder of God's creation. I could see the ocean, all different types of vegetation and various landforms. In my heart, I had a sense of the joy God felt when He formed the world. In the final scene of this ongoing visual movie that played in my mind's eye, I saw a picture of Christ with his hands extended standing beneath a waterfall. Animals of all different species, birds, deer, monkeys—everything imaginable—emerged from where His hands were extended and filled the earth.

By the time the vision was complete, I was literally shaking because of the vivid images and power of God's presence. For the days following the vision, I had the most unusual experience. I could actually hear creation glorifying God. At times, it was so loud it was nearly deafening. We would drive along the mountainous roads outside Honduras' capital city, and I could hear every piece of creation cry out, "Glory, Glory, Glory." The trees, the mountains, the cows in the pasture, the clouds in the sky were all crying "glory" to God. Things you would never consider—mud puddles, gravel, brown grass—were crying "glory" to God with equal fervency. Through this experience, I realized one of my greatest purposes in life is to join with creation crying "Glory, Glory, Glory" with my mouth, heart, strength, and life.

After three days, the crying of creation within my spirit slowly abated. In the following weeks, I began reading Scriptures with a new understanding. Luke 19:37-40 says:

> When he came near the place where the road goes down the Mount of Olives, the whole crowd of disciples began joyfully to praise God in loud voices for all the miracles they had seen: "Blessed is the king who comes in the name of the Lord!"
>
> "Peace in heaven and glory in the highest!"
>
> Some of the Pharisees in the crowd said to Jesus, "Teacher, rebuke your disciples!"
>
> "I tell you," he replied, "if they keep quiet, the stones will cry out."

After my experience, I realized Jesus wasn't kidding around. The very rocks of the earth would cry out. In fact, I believe they already are. We just can't always hear them.

I also began reading Romans 8, where Paul speaks of creation "groaning," in a new light and depth of understanding. I finally grasped how the four living creatures John describes in the worship around the throne never cease saying, "Holy, holy, holy is the Lord God Almighty, who was, and is, and is to come" (REVELATION 4:8). Such few words for all of eternity are more than enough.

The experience also gave me a deeper revelation of Christ's presence and involvement in creation. The Genesis account is chocked full of so many "God said" and "God made" that it's easy to forget Christ was there, too. In Genesis 1:26, it says, "Then God said, 'Let us make man in our image, in our likeness'" (emphasis added). The same Christ who walked the earth is the same one who was part of forming the earth and filling it with life.

Though the vision is now years behind me, I'll be out hiking from time to time and hear the quiet whisper of "Glory, Glory, Glory" within my spirit; it's a reminder of God's presence, glory, and dominion throughout the earth.

This type of experience moves me from having knowledge of God in my head to having knowledge of God in my heart. I know more about Him. I see His presence in new ways. I am not alone. I live in a generation that is hungry for God.

This generation is spiritually starved for His presence. We want to know Him, and we want to be around people who know Him.

If we are going to be God's people and part of His kingdom, then we have to know Him. We must have more than information about God to offer, we must have God dwelling within us. When people come to us seeking answers, we must offer them more than pat answers or religious clichés.

More information is available to this generation than any other in the history of the world. Developments in numerous fields—scientific, historical, philosophical, technological—result in countless articles which include new facts, statistics, quotes, and trends. Yet when most people ask questions about God, they aren't looking for information. If they did, they could go online or visit a library. They want to talk to someone who knows Him.

If you wanted to know about the President, would you rather

speak with a person who read a book about the President or a person who had dinner with the President last week at the White House? Which would you choose? Most people would choose to hear the details of the dinner engagement. After all, you could hear about the book some other time or pick up your own copy. But dinner with the President! This person could share intimate details like what the President likes to eat, what the White House dining room looks like, what the President was wearing, what's it like to be with him, and maybe tell a funny story or two.

Most people will choose to spend time with someone who has intimate knowledge of God over someone who just knows some information about Him. This generation wants to be around people who know God and have heard from Him. They want to be around people who don't just know God's principles but who have paid a price, walked them out, and have born fruit through their faithfulness.

How can we become the people of God that we are intended to be? By learning to hear and obey God's voice.

May God whispers become a part of your everyday.

SOURCES

1 Cowman, L.B. *Streams in the Desert.* (Grand Rapids: Zondervan, 1997), p. 83. Taken from *Streams in the Desert.* Copyright 1997 by Zondervan Publishing House. Used by permission of Zondervan.

2 Metzger, Doug. *Liberty Through The Cross.* (Self-published, 2000), p. 96-97.

3 Ibid., p. 70.

4 Ibid., p. 71-72.

»

from
God Whispers

Margaret Feinberg is a writer based in Steamboat Springs, Colorado. She has written for a variety of nationally recognized magazines and is a contributing writer to *Enjoying God* and *I AM RELEVANT.*

There's More to Life Than Romance, Money and Poker

«

By Jason Boyett

Three Stories

» **One:** Motivational guru Zig Ziglar tells of a memorable revival service led by early twentieth-century evangelical firebrand Mordecai Ham, who is perhaps best known for being the preacher on the night of Billy Graham's conversion. One evening, before taking the podium to deliver his typically fire-and-brimstone sermon, Ham was approached by a stranger. The man pulled the preacher aside and said, "Mr. Ham, I'm here because I'm curious. But I just want you to know that I don't believe in heaven, I don't believe in hell, I don't believe in God and I certainly don't believe in prayer."

Ham thanked him for his honesty and stepped onto the stage. He addressed the large crowd. "Folks, we've got an unusual man at our service tonight. He doesn't believe in heaven, doesn't believe in hell, doesn't believe in God, and certainly doesn't believe in prayer. So I want all of us, the entire time I'm preaching, to pray that God will kill this man before I'm through."

As soon as the words left Ham's mouth, the non-believer leapt violently from his seat and elbowed his way past his fellow congregants into the aisle. He sprinted toward the door and burst out of the building, all the while screaming at the top of his lungs, "No! No! Don't you do it! Don't pray that! Please, don't you do it!"[1]

Everyone believes in something.

Two: In the early nineties, when I was in high school, my grandfather Brownie was diagnosed with laryngeal cancer. A malignant tumor was discovered on his voice box. Due to the strength of the disease, only one real solution was offered—a total laryngectomy.

So they took his voice away.

After having the larynx removed, patients can learn to speak again by pursuing a couple of options. The first is to use a mechanical or artificial larynx, a device held up to the permanent hole in the neck (called a stoma) that remains following the operation. The device converts air vibrations into sound. You can understand someone who speaks with a mechanical larynx, but they sound like an inflectionless robot.

Option two involved learning to talk in a completely new way, via esophageal speech. It's accomplished by gulping air into the top of the esophagus and then forcing it back out—speech by way of a glorified burp. The burp vibrates the walls of the throat, producing sound that's shaped into words as it travels through the mouth. Esophageal speech is difficult to master and the resulting sound is low-pitched and gruff. But you can inflect it, and it's all your own.

Brownie tried the mechanical larynx for a few days but hated it. So he chose door number two, and went to work. After a grueling year, he'd taught himself to talk again. And to sing. And even to laugh.

You need to know this about my grandfather: He's the very definition of a tough old coot.[2] My memories of Brownie before his cancer surgery are of a hard-working, secretly kind but outwardly stern retiree, one whose demeanor befitted an ex-Marine military policeman, which he was. But after the surgery, during the process of learning to speak, the most surprising thing happened—over the course of the most difficult year of his life, Brownie's outward disposition did a 180.

I first recognized it one evening playing Ping-Pong with him.[3] He slammed the ball at me, it bounced off my chest, I made a face, and Brownie laughed. Not a regular laugh, but an esophageal one—an exaggerated wheeze. Not content with the primal release of the wheeze-laugh, Brownie switched to a physical one. He doubled over at the waist and started slapping his knee, his face lit with a denture-rich grin. Then he slapped the table, wagged his head, slapped the knee one more time, wheezed again, and finally straightened back up.

Brownie had just executed a full-body laugh. And from that point on, he became the most enjoyable laugher I've ever been around. I honestly don't remember him expressing much amusement before the surgery; I'm certain he didn't laugh near as much then as he does now. Brownie's life is a lot funnier these days, and when something tickles him, you know it. The raspy laugh hisses out from deep inside him, like a burst of air from a leaky tire; then the knee-slapping kicks in. His internal joy wells up into an external burst of movement, and it's wonderful to see. It never fails to make me grin.

Three: In 1946, Dr. Percy Spencer, a self-taught engineer with the Raytheon Corporation, was testing a new vacuum tube called a magnetron during a radar-related research project. During the test, he felt a strange sensation, and reaching into the pocket nearest the magnetron, he discovered that the candy bar he'd placed there had completely melted. This intrigued him, so he did an experiment. He held a bag of unpopped popcorn kernels near the tube. They popped.

Another test the next day: Spencer and a curious colleague placed an egg next to the magnetron tube. They watched as the egg began to shiver and wobble, a result of pressure against the shell caused by the egg's rapidly rising internal temperature. Suddenly the egg exploded, spraying hot yolk onto their faces.

Spencer, widely regarded as an electronics genius, figured out what was happening. The energy of the low-density radio waves emitted by the magnetron were agitating the water molecules in the food products, making them vibrate and spin. The molecular gyrations caused friction. The friction generated heat. As opposed to a range oven—which cooks food slowly from the outside—Spencer had discovered a way to heat things up internally, and to do it much faster. He soon harnessed those magnetron waves into something usable, then gave his invention a name: the "radar range." Today we call it the microwave oven.[4]

We all believe in something. And like a knee-slapping wheeze laugh or an explosion of yolk, that interior belief will eventually make its way to the surface. The inside can't stay inside for long, and the quality of that heat makes us who we are. Such is the case for religion—or as it's known in our dogmaphobic society: spirituality.

Here in the technology-driven infancy of the twenty-first century, the quest for the spiritual has reached a weird juncture. Church attendance has held steady over the last few years, as 43 percent of American adults attends a church or religious service during a typical week. Yet, according to the Barna Research Group, more than one out of every five adults under the age of thirty-five consider themselves to be agnostic, atheistic, or affiliated with a non-Christian faith—a percentage that's more than two times higher than that of our parents' generation.[5]

Those numbers tell us a couple of things. First of all, we can assume that young adults don't necessarily equate "spiritual" with "Christian." While generations of Americans before us operated within a strictly Christian worldview, that's not so today. Christianity is only one of many viable faiths to our informed, open-minded society, and is being treated as such.

Second, young adults are exhibiting a growing interest in spirituality, but are looking for it outside the typical church structure. Smack in the middle of a suffocatingly materialistic culture, we're still on a quest for meaning and purpose—but that search is now much more expansive. We're exploring new faiths and challenging old ones. The reason for this is obvious: the old guard has failed to satisfy.

It's at this point that I should reveal that, yes, I am a member of the old guard. I am a Christian. I am a believer.

What do I believe in? Plenty. I believe the sun's going to come up in the morning. I believe the chair I'm sitting in will support me until I stand. I believe in the power of my body to keep itself going—heart beating, liver functioning, lungs breathing for at least another fifty years or so—and that I'll awaken from my next sleep. I believe in the authenticity of my daughter's hugs, and that the flash in my newborn son's eyes is the light of recognition. He knows me.

I believe in God. He knows me, too.

At times it can be a difficult belief, one that doesn't come as easily to me as it did when I was younger. It's challenged on a daily basis by the injustice of our fellow humans and the ridiculousness of the religious, by the prevalence of unmitigated evil and uninhibited disaster. Ten years ago, my faith was the simple assurance that the Judeo-Christian Jehovah, as revealed in the person of Christ, was and is absolutely real. Today, on a good day, I still hold to that. But on a bad day? On a bad day, faith for me is living as if God's real, but...wondering.

Mine is a limping, bandaged version of Christianity, one that is more likely to wince at the weirdness of my faith than embrace it. I'm not amused by American Christianity's rising irrelevance, its gradual movement to the fringes of culture while, nevertheless, attempting to appropriate the music and entertainment and marketing strategies and political tactics of that very culture for its own use. I'm no fan of the way we try to impose man's structures on God, because I seriously doubt He's just a glorified, holy version of the white Republican male. I'm tired of the bullheaded dogmatism of the evangelical church and its increasingly misguided priorities[6]—but despite the baggage, the Christian church is a foundational part of my life.

It's flawed and ugly and, often, just plain wrong. The thing is, so am I.

That's why the church remains my home. It's where I live.

So my wobbly faith remains in place, hanging at times by a thread, but still, somehow, attached. My faith is something I hope to model for my kids, just like my parents and grandparents before me. It is the common ground that connects me to my closest friends. It's the tingle I get when standing thigh-deep in southwest Colorado's Cebolla Creek, surrounded by God's playground of Aspen and silence and wary trout. It's the invisible backbone to the earlier chapters on generosity and selflessness and optimism and even romance.

It's what gives my life meaning—and that's what most of our human pursuits ultimately come down to: the search for meaning, the reach for significance, the hunt for wisdom. Why? Because I firmly believe there's more to Jason Boyett than blood and flesh and bone and nerves and gray matter. I have to think that we're not just here to procreate and survive and get bigger and better and stronger as a race, that there's more to life than staying alive as long as possible. That things like joy and grief and contentment are more than just chemical reactions and firing synapses—though, undoubtedly, biology has *something* to do with it—but that they are connected to something greater. A "deeper magic," as C.S. Lewis called it in *The Lion, the Witch and the Wardrobe*.

I have to believe we each have a soul.

And if we have a soul, then another question follows, this one more difficult: What for? An easier question to answer is the converse: If there's no such thing as the soul, then what the hell are we living for? If it all ends in nothingness, then what's the point?

Which brings us to the title of this chapter. We've dedicated a bunch of pages to discussion of things we ought to be aware of at this juncture in life. Some have been marginally serious, others practical, a few downright silly. But none are the end-all of existence. Making wise financial decisions won't guarantee a fulfilling life—there are too many rich people funding psychiatrists to support that theory. Love, sex, and dating? They can make you feel warm and fuzzy—but warm and fuzzy are poor combatants against hardship. Poker? Groceries? A decent résumé? Not a chance.

The thing that gets us through life is hope. Hope that we're right about the soul thing. Hope that life's tiny coincidences and pockets of emotion are evidence of something greater. Hope that the light at the end of the tunnel isn't an oncoming train.

Hope that this confusion we feel—this confusion I feel about who's behind the curtain, about the nature of coincidence and the glory of fly-fishing and the light in my kids' eyes—that these are, in themselves, the evidence of God. And, to paraphrase St. Augustine of Hippo, "Why worry about understanding? If you think you understand it, it's not God."[7]

The questions, the lack of understanding, the uncertainty, the search for God—these are what make us human. They are the microwaves that get our molecules to spinning. They agitate us. They cause internal friction. The process is not always comfortable, but it does lead to change, and change is good. The eventual release of internal pressure, like hot yolk bursting through a cracked shell, is a soothing act of destruction. It makes things feel right again.

That's why, despite the discomfort, I keep putting myself as close to the microwaves as I can. That's where the heat is. That's where the soul begins. That's faith.

And that faith led me headlong into the person of Jesus Christ, whom we Christians believe to be the incarnation of God: Jehovah dressed in a suit of His own creation. I don't get what Jesus says a lot of the time—and I'm not alone, based on the number of Christian denominations in the world, each claiming a different understanding of the Scriptures—but I generally like it. I like the anti-establishment parables He told, the way He got the angriest with the pious religious people and showed kindness to the drunks and prostitutes and lepers. I like the way He chose a dozen uneducated, incapable commoners and occasional nitwits to become His disciples.[8] I like the way He seemed to treat children and women as equals in a male-dominated world, and how His social teachings were always wrapped around selflessness and humility and giving and unconditional love—relational ideas that were so unusual at that time and in that place. And I like the way He offered grace and forgiveness and mercy with no strings attached.

I like that most of all.

When my grandfather lost his larynx, he lost the mechanism to do the stuff that once came so naturally. Singing. Speaking. Laughing. Disease stripped them away, and all that remained was an empty throat. The stirring was still there—he still had the words inside him, he still had the capacity for joy—but the mechanism for releasing them was gone. He had to relearn those things. He had to remake his voice and his laugh and his song with the damaged scraps he had left.

Now his raspy voice is even sweeter. Brownie's laughing is not only more frequent, but more enjoyable, because it's a fight his whole body commits to in a flurry of wheezing, knee-slapping, waist-bending fury. Each laugh is a battle, but when it finally gets to the surface? It's good.

Brownie's story is also the Christian one: a natural Eden spoiled by the disease of sin; the emptiness of the sin waging a violent conflict with the longing of the soul; the deeper magic struggling toward the light. In Christ, we find the new mechanism for release. We find a new way to talk, to laugh, to sing. It often requires more of us than we'd like to give—in a fallen world, life is harder than it was intended to be, more complicated than necessary—but the end result is a spiritual body laugh.

And achieving that laugh? *That* is what we're after.

All of us believe in something; all of us need a little religion. And a lot of religions have much to offer the world. The postmodern, all-inclusive thing to do would be to say they're all virtually the same, just multiple paths to a single destination. That may be true—

like I said, for every one rock-solid answer I have about my faith, I have a dozen other squishy questions—but I'm not ready to concede that yet.

Because from where I am, the burden of Christian faith—in all its frustrating, misunderstood, Left Behind-reading glory—seems to make the most sense. It gives me hope. It offers meaning. It stirs my soul. It heats me up, wheezes from me in a guttural laugh, and occasionally bursts from my shell in a blast of yolk.

It's important, at least to me, so I thought you should know about it. That's all.

SOURCES

1 Zig Ziglar, *Success for Dummies* (Foster City, CA: IDG Books Worldwide, 1998), 190.

2 For instance, at the age of seventy, Brownie was mowing his lawn when he accidentally fell over a six-foot retaining wall. He landed headfirst on the top of his shoulder and blasted his rotator cuff to pieces. So what did he do? He finished mowing. Then he went inside and carried on with his business. Several days later, he finally went to the doctor because he couldn't lift his arm over his head to get dressed. It wasn't that big of a deal, he told us at the time—just inconvenient.

3 He used to defeat me regularly when I was in high school. Now, at eighty, the guy still beats me four out of five times, and I'm a pretty decent table tennis player.

4 Don Murray, "Percy Spencer and His Itch to Know," *Reader's Digest*, August 1958, 114.

5 "American Faith is Diverse, as Shown Among Five Faith-Based Segments," *Barna Research Online* (posted January 9, 2002, at www.barna.org/cgi-bin/PagePressRelease.asp?PressReleaseID=105&Reference=B).

6 Like focusing too intently on political issues like school prayer, social issues like homosexuality, or eschatological issues like the Second Coming—at the expense of immediate needs like hunger and poverty.

7 St. Augustine of Hippo, *Sermons* (Sermon 117,5: PL 38,673).

8 Which, to my mind, is akin to President Bush asking Carrot Top to serve as one of his closest advisors.

»

from
Things You Should Know By Now

Jason Boyett is the co-author of *Cheap Ways To...* and the creative director for a design and communications company in Amarillo, Texas. A musician, artist, and writer, his work has appeared in a variety of print and online publications.

Cheap Ways to Help the Needy

By Jason Boyett

"Give a man a fish and he'll eat for a day. Teach a man to fish and he'll eat for a lifetime." No doubt you've heard the axiom before. It's often used to condemn no-strings-attached giving to the poor. Cliché or not, it paints a nice picture. Unfortunately, it only paints half the picture—it's great to teach a man to fish, but if the man has no fishing gear and no water nearby, how do you expect the knowledge of *how* to fish to do anything for him?

That's the plight of the poor. As it is for millions of people across the planet, poverty is a problem in the United States as well. The 2000 U.S. Census indicated that more than thirty million Americans live below the poverty line. Nearly half of those are children. And while dealing with the problem of poverty involves "helping the poor to help themselves," we need to remember that such a solution is long-term. What are we to do in the short-term? It's far too easy to get caught up in the politics and methodology of helping the poor while forgetting that you can contribute something yourself. In fact, a number of recent surveys have indicated that today's younger generation gives less to charity than any previous generation. Is it because we don't care? Or is it because we think someone else ought to be doing it—someone like Bill Gates, who could feed and shelter every homeless person in America for a month without making a dent in his wallet?

Did you pay for this book? If so, it's doubtful you fall below the poverty line. Most likely, you have something to give. You can't alleviate the problem by yourself; no one can. But what you can do is distribute some grace to your corner of the world. The thing to remember is that helping the poor isn't just about donating money. It's about meeting needs. Here's what you can do:

HOMELESS SHELTERS

If you live in a city of any size, there is probably at least one homeless shelter that helps people with meals, beds, hygiene, and other services. Most shelters welcome volunteers for a number of activities, from preparing and distributing meals to working in the business office.

FOOD BANKS

Surveys have indicated up to 40 percent of people serviced by community food banks have, at one time or another, had to decide between eating and paying rent. If that's a decision you've never had to make, why not find a way to help out? Community food banks are instrumental in assisting the poor in your community, particularly around the holidays. They employ volunteers to sort and collect salvaged food (much of which comes from area supermarkets), distribute bread, manage inventory, and perform office tasks. You can help by doing any of the above, or by organizing and giving to inventory builders like canned food drives.

SWEATERS

A few years ago, the inspirational magazine *Guideposts* came up with a unique way to help the poor—knitting sweaters for them. Over the last four years, more than 120,000 children's sweaters have been knitted by volunteers in the U.S., Canada, Australia, and even New Guinea. If you can knit or crochet, *Guideposts* will be happy to give you a pattern. Don't know how to knit? They'll even hook you up with instructions. For more on the project, check out *www.guideposts.org*.

HABITAT FOR HUMANITY

Since 1976, Habitat has built in excess of 100,000 simple houses across the world for families lacking adequate shelter. A non-denominational, non-profit organization, Habitat sells its houses via interest-free mortgages. The homes are built by the homeowners themselves and a team of volunteers. If you have any sort of construction, electrical, or plumbing skills, you're exactly the kind of volunteer help Habitat needs. For those who don't know a Philips from a flathead, Habitat projects provide a fun, unintimidating environment to learn—all the while helping a very appreciative family. Contact your local chapter, or visit *www.habitat.org.*

CLOTHING & NECESSITIES

Most of us have far too many clothes—in our closet, stuff we haven't worn in years. When you run out of space, resist the urge to sell your old clothing on consignment or in garage sales. Instead, donate it to a charity like the Salvation Army or its equivalent. My wife and I worked one weekend a few years ago with a downtown women's center, the kind of place where battered women stay until they get their lives back together. We discovered the center was always in need of decent women's clothing, in addition to baby supplies and kids' clothes. After that weekend, Aimee cleaned out her closet immediately. If you have a full closet or baby clothes you'll never use again, why not give them to someone who'll treasure them?

BE THOUGHTFUL

It's easy in today's society to ignore the wizened drifters holding "Will Work for Food" signs at busy intersections. You can't help every single person with a cardboard sign, but it's inhuman to pretend not to see them each and every time you hit a stoplight. I know many kind people who just don't feel right about giving money to the homeless, worrying that they may be paying for an alcohol addiction or their next drug fix. But the truly compassionate still find a way to give. I know of one elderly lady who has begun collecting coupons or gift certificates for free meals at local restaurants. She keeps them in the ashtray of her car, and is happy to pass them along to the hungry. Once, my sister, who was sixteen at the time, was moved to tears by the sight of a small family on the street corner with a sign that read, simply, "hungry." She had no cash on her, but told the family to wait five minutes. She sped home and made peanut-butter-and-jelly sandwiches out of an entire loaf of bread, shoved the sandwiches back into the bread sack, and returned to the family. Tears were shed on their end, too.

BE KIND

If you have a chance to interact with the needy, make a point to talk to them like you would any individual—your neighbor, a business associate, a family member. Often, there's no better gift than the feeling of worth and civilization they feel when someone treats them like a real person. I once read a newspaper feature on the homeless, in which one of the individuals profiled said something I'll always remember: "You don't think I feel like crap when a generous person takes me into a restaurant and feeds me? Here I am in the clothes I wore yesterday and smelling like trash. But you can take my mind off that by speaking nicely to me and not looking down on me."

The poor aren't just looking for money. They're looking for understanding, significance, a human connection—gifts to which no dollar amount applies.

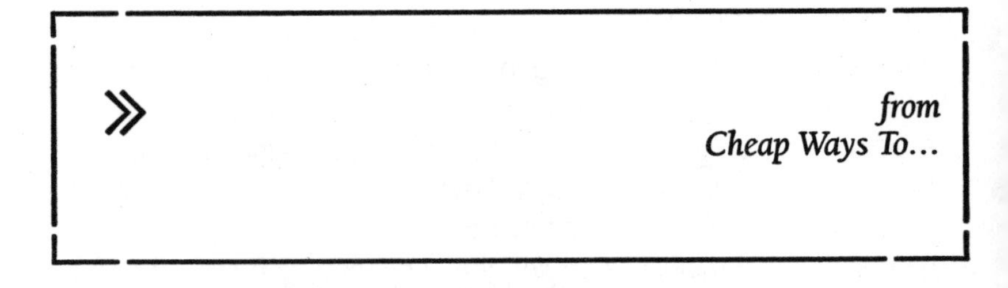

Jason Boyett is the co-author of *Cheap Ways To ...* and the creative director for a design and communications company in Amarillo, Texas. A musician, artist, and writer, his work has appeared in a variety of print and online publications.

CHEAP WAYS TO LIVE BENEATH YOUR MEANS

BY KATIE MEIER

If you're like me, you don't consider yourself a consumer glutton. You don't own the road with your pimped-out Excursion. You don't own the neighborhood with your seven-bedroom mansion. Nope, you're just a little piece of the American pie. You take in a few dinners and movies with your friends, you drive whatever you can afford--and will get you there–and when you splurge it's rarely on a private jet or a gold-plated hot tub.

But whether we buy the bling-bling or the boring, we need to recognize that we all have the potential to become consumer gluttons. To live a life below our means is less about the amount we consume than knowing what our limits of consumption are, or what they should be. Best the prototypical picture of a life lived in debt and beyond your budget by checking out the advice below.

KEEP RECEIPTS

Consider keeping receipts cheap therapy, as it works in two annoyingly effective ways: (1) It's a big-ole pain. The more we're forced to endure the asking, collecting, and saving that go with stashing receipts, the more aware we're forced to become about our spending. (2) It's a running tally right in front of our face. It will only take a few receipts to tell how closely related we're becoming to Sir Elton (Did I mention his bankruptcy problems?).

CULTIVATE CONSCIOUSNESS

To become conscious spenders, here's what we need to do: take the aforementioned advice about receipts, and get realistic about earning versus spending.

First, take one week and actually keep receipts from all the stuff you buy and all the bills you pay. Second, get out the calculator, sit down with a cold beverage (you kept the receipt for that beverage, right?), relax, and add up the damage. Next, find your last paycheck and divide this amount (by two or four) to understand exactly how much you make each week of your life. Last, and most magical of all, compare the total you spend with the total you pull in.

Doing this over the course of one month will likely walk you straight into the honest fact that you're overspent and using credit to cover you. A change in lifestyle costs nothing and can have you living within your means in no time.

FORGET LUMP-SUM LIVING

Do envelopes, do a money program, do whatever, just abandon a life lived by the lump-sum balance in your bankbook. Lump-sum living is too tempting and too vague, a sure sign of something that might lead us away from a life lived under our means. Instead, introduce (dut da da da!) "Spending Sectors" into your life. From CDs to collectibles, from groceries to Grande Mochaccinos, spending sectors make you a diva of divvying funds, and at the same time set limits on spending. Set sector limits by allocating funds to each. Spending is fine, but sectors clear up the picture and keep you from capitalizing on the longings only lump-sum living can provide.

CHEAP OUT ON THE EVERYDAY

Though we use some services over and over everyday, we rarely check back over time to insure that we're still getting a good deal. If you still think a free toaster is what banking is all about, it's time to get with the times, pop. Check your bank, phone, insurance, cable, cell, and other service providers to be sure you're getting the cheapest rates, rather than paying inflated fees for old school options, services, or allocations of coverage. In addition, get your head out of the clouds with regard to your real life; though the 1977 Nissan might be a superstar in your eyes, premium gas and that weekly wash and wax can bend a budget to the max over the course of time. Let items absorb costs appropriate to their stature and with regard to the reality of your means.

DON'T KEEP UP WITH THE JONESES

They might have the tight ride and the sweet crib, but they're likely in debt and living well beyond their means. End the rivalry of ridiculous stuff by providing for yourself what you can afford and no more. Learn from the wisdom of pop music here and realize, "It's not having what you want, it's wanting what you've got."

LEARN ABOUT DEBT RATIOS

Living below our means might seem to have everything to do with saving, but it's actually about learning how to spend with some precision; after all, from college degrees to cul-de-sac homes, there will always be a few things nearly everyone will have to go into debt in order to provide. Thus, living below our means when carrying debt has to do with understanding how much debt we can take on—too much debt and our budget will bend so far out of whack we'll think we're a bunch of old ladies trying to do the electric slide.

Figure your "debt ratio" to see if your budget is becoming "loaned out," so to speak, by having taken on too many creditors. Because a debt ratio is just your total monthly debt payments divided by your monthly income, it's easy to figure. Anything more than 40 percent is a sign you're likely in too deep to maintain a life below your means and could be headed for a serious financial fiasco soon.

SUGGESTIONS WILLY-NILLY

Make a wish list of items and ask for them as gifts to cut costs. Pay for things that are planned or necessary expenses only by making emergencies, extras, and seasonal splurges a part of your regular budget, not an afterthought you afford through credit. Impose a waiting period on all major purchases rather than falling prey to impulse buying, and save for the item bit-by-bit while you wait. Don't buy on credit; if you do, write a check for the cost and deduct it from your account that same day to be certain you don't let interest get the better of you when you can't pay the balance at the end of the month.

» *from Cheap Ways To...*

Katie Meier and her husband live in the southwest while she completes a master's in religion.

God at the Movies

By Gareth Higgins

»

Going to the cinema can be a spiritual experience akin to worship, which can inspire and convict as well as any sermon. So, let's remind ourselves of a few of cinema's worshipers. St. Francis of Assisi is my favorite saint (if you're allowed to rank them). For some unknown reason, in 1972, Franco Zeffirelli decided to make a Francis biopic, *Brother Sun, Sister Moon*, and I'm glad that he did. While the film is clearly bound in the 1970s—it fit the culture of hippydom and free love—Francis is portrayed for what he was: a single minded lover of God, servant of the poor, and steward of nature. The scene where he announces his conversion to his rich father and all the people of his town by stripping naked in the square is a wonderful example of how God uses the foolish things to shame the wise. Would we recognize the deep spirituality of such madness, or would we react as Francis' father did, with humiliated self-protection, if it were to happen today?

Ben-Hur had more of a sense of decorum, but that film's respect for Christ is honorable. We never see Christ's face, and although he is a little de-humanized, the film encourages an appropriate sense of awe. (Useless trivia: Leslie Nielson from *The Naked Gun* auditioned for the role of Judah Ben-Hur's best friend, the Roman soldier Messala. Oh, how things could have been so different...) Andrei Tarkovsky was one of cinema's greatest poets. His Russian films don't appeal to the kind of audience that wants its information *FAST*, but his was a true mystic cinema. The experience of God that enfolds us in his films is unmatched elsewhere. I recommend you start with *Andrei Rublev*, about an icon artist in the middle ages. Words cannot begin to describe the power of this film; it is almost a religious icon in itself. *Signs* fits here as well, because its story is more about the healing of broken faith in God as it is about scary little aliens in the backyard. Its ending is a little too neat for me, and its answers too tight, but I cannot deny that it helped my faith at a low point. Perhaps it will do the same for you.

You might also find spiritual solace in films about the grace of God. *Chocolat* is quite similar to *Babette's Feast* in that it's about a stranger coming to an isolated village and bringing strange foodstuffs. But it takes on the power of legalistic religion more directly, and perhaps is the weaker for it. It's still a wonderful film, and there is one moment—when the weak priest finally summons the strength to say what he really believes—when you might want to applaud aloud. He cautions his people against judging others, saying: "Don't let your goodness be defined by what you don't do; or your community by who you exclude, but by what and whom you embrace." There is a hilarious, beautiful, and deeply moving example of this, when the Pharisaic mayor gorges himself on chocolate. He lies like a baby on a mound of sweet heaven—a better metaphor for what it feels like to be forgiven would be hard to define. There is a glaring flaw, however, because the people of this village ultimately exclude one of their number—an abusive husband. He is not allowed to return. Now, perhaps this is simply a sign that the people have not yet fully understood the implications of grace; they may learn in the future that he should be welcomed back. But, regretfully, I suspect this was an example of political correctness on the part of the filmmakers; forgiveness and grace can only go so far in Hollywood cinema.

Of course, forgiveness and grace go the distance in *It's a Wonderful Life*; this film's appeal seems to be much greater in the U.S.A. than elsewhere, so as a foreigner I won't risk saying too much about it. You've all seen it about twenty times anyway. But it's always worth a repeat visit. *Life is Beautiful* is a more recent parable of grace, where Roberto Benigni protects his son from the trauma of Nazism by inventing a world of safety and games. Some Holocaust survivors have ridiculed this film, saying that concentration camp conditions were so extraordinarily sub-human that nobody would have been able to play along with Benigni's game. Somebody would at least have tried to win favor with the guards by revealing the hidden child. That may be true, and I am not in a place to argue with it. But *Life is Beautiful* is still a magnificent metaphor for good parenting, and for the fact that there may sometimes be a moral imperative to lie.

The key film on grace is based on Victor Hugo's amazing tome *Les Miserables*, which is much more than the reason why the theatre at the top of London's Shaftesbury Avenue is still open. It is too massive a story to be summed up by one theme, but for our purposes, this book is about the Christian community at its best. You all know the story—Valjean, a thief, stays the night at a bishop's house and steals some expensive cutlery before sneaking out in the middle of the night. He is caught and returned to the bishop's house by soldiers, now under the threat of death for his crime. The bishop, instead of agreeing to press charges, greets Valjean with open arms and tear-filled eyes, saying: I'm so glad you returned. You forgot something! Then he gives Valjean his silver candlesticks and insists that the soldiers let him be on his way. And he quietly advises Valjean to use this grace for others. This is nothing less than a sacramental gift of life from the church, a truly Christian act (if by "Christian" we mean the imitation of Christ, which I'm not sure the Church always understands these days). We are, all of us, in need of such grace. And we all, I am sure, are confronted by situations that need our grace. *Les Miserables* reminds us that there is a better way. (There are several film versions, but I most highly recommend the 1995 French version *Les Miserables du Vingtieme Siecle*, which interweaves the story with the Holocaust.)

Grace is often the characteristic most fully embodied by cinematic Christ figures, and they seem to be a dime a dozen these days. So let's just admit that we've all seen *The Matrix* and it inspired us and made us think of the need for a Messiah, etc.

etc. etc. We'll come to that film later. For now, let me encourage you to look beyond the most obvious or well known God-figures in the movies, and sample some of the following:

Maybe the funniest film with a Christ figure at its center is *The Big Lebowski*. I can hear eyebrows raising all over the place now. Has Higgins finally gone mad? I hope not. On first viewing, I just thought this Coen Brothers film was a delightful comedy about nothing much in particular. But then a good friend opened my eyes. The central character is called the Dude, and does very little except hang out, drink copious White Russians, and go to see his friends do performance art. He doesn't work, he doesn't struggle with existentialism, he doesn't get up at a reasonable hour. He just is. As a metaphor for what the Sabbath should really be like, for what the Sabbath is really *for*, the Dude can't be beat, man.

The self-sacrifice of Christ is turned into metaphor in some of the greatest films I know. I find it difficult to convey anything meaningful about these films in mere words, so I won't say very much. *Gandhi* is an obvious choice—a film about the man who imitated the pattern of Jesus, preached regularly from the sermon on the Mount, and, before dying for his cause, said (and I paraphrase): The only people who don't believe that Jesus advocated non-violence are Christians themselves. I would follow Christ if it weren't for the Christians.

Watching *The Prince of Egypt* was the first time I realized that the biblical story of Moses requires him to give up everything—privilege, security, family—before he can be led by God into the desert that will cause him to devote his life to his people. And *The Mission* also leads its characters into a kind of desert—as evangelists in the jungle—where they shall die alongside the original inhabitants at the behest of the corrupt marriage between church and state.

Of course, God as *creator* is found at the movies. I only want to mention two films that evoke our sense of awe at the imagination behind the universe. Luc Bessons' *Atlantis* is a magnificent documentary about life on two-thirds of the earth's surface; there are creatures here that never see the light of day, and Besson does us a service by letting us snoop on their world. Another magisterial piece on the nature of nature is *2001: A Space Odyssey*. Some readers may think this is a strange choice for this chapter on God, as it is usually acclaimed as the greatest humanist tract that cinema has produced. But I think differently (and you would expect me to, wouldn't you?). This film ends with a declaration that there is something "out there" bigger than ourselves; it doesn't make explicit just what that something is, but for me, it has to be divine revelation. The nice thing is, Kubrick always said that he did not want to prescribe for people what his film meant. And he certainly wasn't about to declare a belief in God; so I can say what I like about this one. And, I guess, so can you.

As for the shadow side of religion, controversy, legalism, despair, abuse, and the intolerance of religious institutions come under the cinematic microscope in surprisingly few films. *The Truman Show* imagines the darker implications of Psalm 139 (when it is claimed that God watches our every move) as the main character realizes he is a pawn in a mammoth game, watched over by one man, whose distorted "love" for the character has led him to keep him prisoner. This is what life would be like if God hated us (although I do wish Peter Weir had chosen to end the film on a less acclamatory note). Graham Greene's *The End of the Affair* has been filmed twice; I prefer Neil Jordan's 1999 version, and not just because he's Irish. The story discusses how faith and love are sometimes incompatible, the impossible choice between faith in a God who controls and love for the person that God rejects. It's a powerful piece of cinema that should have been more widely discussed than it was.

There's more "bad religion" in *Priest*, where issues of sexuality, integrity, honesty, and grace are examined in painful detail. How the Church so often seems to fail to deal graciously with reality was exemplified when this film was almost denied a U.S. release because of protests from Christians. Don't people realize that they need to face these issues rather than brush them away like flies? Unfortunately, these issues will not be dead in the winter; they are with us all year round and cannot be gotten rid of with insect repellent.

Finally, and appropriately, I bring you the "end-times," and here we need a note on terminology. "Apocalypse" *does not mean the end of the world.* It means "revelation." Francis Coppola has made some wonderful contributions to popular culture, but he, probably more than anyone, has helped us misunderstand that term. Apocalypse is a word used to refer to the revealing of something that could not be seen before. It is a misnomer to apply it to the end-times. Now we've got that out of the way, let's get down to the doom of the end. There's a lot of doom in *The Rapture*, a little-seen film from the mid-'90s, illustrating pre-millennial tension among the middle class. One of the characters doesn't get what she prayed for and becomes terribly angry toward God. The anger seeps into her soul to the extent where she refuses to enter heaven when she dies. It's a shocking evocation of how rage can destroy us. And it's both more honest, and an infinitely better work than the psychologically-suspect, scripturally-ambiguous run of end-times films and books that have recently colonized the North American popular Christian consciousness. Some of the end-times anxiety I've encountered among Christians is borderline cultic, and we might do well to look at Jane Campion's *Holy Smoke* for a lesson. It's a splendidly witty story about a "cult de-programmer" who gets seduced by one of his subjects in the desert. Like so many of us, he simply does not know what he's doing. Thankfully, Tarkovsky knew what *he* was doing when he made *The Sacrifice*, a surreal spiritual journey on the cusp of the world's end. He was also responsible for the first film of Stanislaw Lem's novel *Solaris*, where a man is visited by the dream of his dead wife and offered the opportunity to stay with the unreal dream, or to return to the sadness of truth. Steven Soderbergh filmed another version of the book, which I actually prefer (sorry, film fans, I have to be wrong sometimes), in which Mr. Clooney got to really act, and we encounter something akin to what heaven might be like. One of the versions has the central character simply waiting, while in the other, he finds what he's looking for. When he asks, "Am I alive or dead?" the answer comes back, "We don't have to think like that anymore." It proposes that there are no answers, only choices. To choose God above all else, when the chips are down, when the evidence is against us, to hope for something bigger than ourselves, to muster faith that what we have believed is real, to recall the times when we actually *did* believe it... The power of these films about God is that, at their best, they transport us into a Presence we don't understand, but that we know we need. It's not quite the same thing as a transcendent moment in a cathedral, as the pipe organ swells, the incense intoxicates our senses, and the congregation experiences a moment of oneness unparalleled elsewhere. But it's not totally different either.

from
How Movies Helped Save My Soul

Gareth Higgins, 27, is an academic, freelance writer and research consultant specializing in Northern Ireland affairs, religion, peacemaking, film and post-modern culture. He often appears on BBC Radio Ulster politics and religious affairs programs.

GRACE

BY STEVE STOCKMAN

Bono often has said it is his Catholic guilt that drives him. Just as this is another veil to protect him from being labeled in any particular camp—he asked if the pope was aware he wasn't a Catholic before he met him—there is truth in the statement. It is Bono's spiritual provocation that will not allow him to lie back and enjoy his own luxury. His obsession with Jesus Christ prods him to keep stirring up anything he can to improve the world. As he told Olaf Tyaransen in a Hot Press interview in November 2000: "I can't live with acquiescence. I can't make peace with myself or the world. I just can't. To me, it's like rolling over. So in doing things like Jubilee 2000, I do feel better for actually feeling that I'm getting my hands around the throat of something I care about."[1]

That idea of grace that Bono mentioned as a theology for Jubilee 2000 has been a constant phrase on the lips of Bono in more recent years. Bono even sent a copy of Philip Yancey's book *What's So Amazing About Grace* to Oasis' Noel Gallagher after the two had an in-depth conversation about faith in 2001. In a *Q* article just before the release of *All That You Can't Leave Behind*, Bono says he was always more into grace than karma.[2] If karma was what it was all about, he was coming back as a frog! Sean O'Hagan, in his detailed article on the events of the Belfast Agreement Yes concert, says Bono was chatting with Unionist politician David Trimble about the merits of the hymn "Amazing Grace." Even before that, when asked by British broadcaster and television celebrity Chris Evans what song he would sing if the world was about to end, Bono immediately responded "Amazing Grace," and continued, "how sweet the sound." Then there is the final song on *All That You Can't Leave Behind*, "Grace": "It's the name for a girl/ It's also a thought that changed the world." In concert from here on, Bono would name check "Amazing Grace" neatly into the lyrics of "I Will Follow." That makes an interesting dovetailing of the U2 career, as "I Will Follow" was the first track on the band's first album, and "Grace" was the final track on U2's most recent album at that point.

The spirit of this grace came through in an interview Bono did with Irish journalist Joe Jackson about a Samuel Beckett Film Festival at the beginning of 2001 in Dublin. Jackson touched on the underlying sense of attitude within the U2 camp, as its decade hidden behind the shades of irony faded and gave birth to yet another reinvention.[3] Throughout the interview, Jackson constantly tried to caress and collide Beckett and Bono with each other. Under the surmise that these two Irish writers are very strange bedfellows, he probed Bono to conclude that they have nothing in common. As with the vast majority of interviews with Bono, the God question was raised, and Jackson pointed out that it's a godless universe that Beckett depicts and this must leave Bono cold. "No, it doesn't because a lot of my friends are atheists," he responded. "It's lukewarm believers that drive me out of the Church. It's the big questions, isn't it? If there's a God, it's serious; if there's not a God, it's even more serious. And Beckett did at least approach the question."[4] Bono's respect for the atheist is refreshing. Many believers distance themselves from those with differing views on God, sometimes even within different churches. Bono makes them his friends and then makes himself accountable to them. He has fellowship and sharpens his faith against those with whom he doesn't agree because they are discussing the same issues.

Jackson quoted Beckett as having believed that "to be an artist is to fail as no other dare fail. Failure is his world."[5] Bono immediately responded: "I really identify with that because what I think Beckett is getting at is that you must get the fear of failure out of the way. Once you become a better failure, you can really go places. For example, I have discussed this in the past. The constrictions of being cool. It's useless. And Lou Reed said that to me. He grew up in the fifties with the fifties idea of what it means to be cool. It's a stranglehold." Jackson then asked if U2 had burst beyond that stranglehold. "We played it cool for ten years." Had the band members finally freed themselves to be hot and bothered? "Yeah, we are! But at the start of the nineties, we realized that to touch and reach people during a new decade, we had to come in a different guise. So we did. Now the real challenge is to turn up without a mask. And I must tell you, it's not as easy to take the shades off as I thought it would be."

Here is the secret to the reinvention. The U2 members had lost the need to succeed and had come to terms with being relaxed in failure if failure should come. Isn't this what cool really is? Not minding if the world thinks you are cool. Just being faithful to you, no matter what the consequences. Not that failure was about to descend upon U2. "Beautiful Day" hit number one on the UK charts. The forty-year-olds reigned supreme.

"Beautiful Day" was an interesting opening track for *All That You Can't Leave Behind*. The last track on U2's nineties catalog, as the entire world seemed caught up in a frenzy of apocalyptic doom and gloom, fearful about the ending of a millennium, was "Wake Up Dead Man." It was as though Jesus was in the tomb after his crucifixion, lifeless, with the disciples letting go of all hope. John Lennon's words "the dream is over" come to mind. "Beautiful Day" is like an ecstatic proclamation that Peter and James might have sung just after Mary had come back to the disciples' hiding place with resurrection news. The biblical image used may be the dove going out from the ark to bring back the leaf that informed Noah that the old world had ended and a new one could begin. But even that depicts the whole celebratory mood of dead man waking up and a whole new Kingdom being birthed. The album and the Elevation tour would see a new resurrection shuffle of a mood in the U2 camp.

As well as the biblical reference in "Beautiful Day" and the band's theological take on "Grace," the whole album is drenched in an upfront spirituality. The cover even has a clue as to the state of U2's spiritual temperature as it features a cryptic Bible verse from Jeremiah 33:3. The band had gotten Steve Averill to doctor the cover shot of the band members taken at Charles De Gaule Airport and change the gate number behind them to read J33-3. Bono called the verse God's telephone number as it reads, "Call to me and I will answer you and tell you great and unsearchable things you do not know."

That cover shot of the band members in a place of departure with their baggage beside them and Bono checking his passport depicts traveling. Symbolically, the music was leaving in other directions, and the technology was staying behind. There has to be more, though, and "Walk On" gives an obvious clue with a clever twist and a familiar phrase, "You're packing your suitcase for a place none of us has been/ A place that has to be believed to be seen." The song, dedicated to Burmese human rights campaigner Aung San Suu Kyi, does seem to live in two dimensions. Bono is always running and climbing and crawling toward what he is looking for here on earth. A world of freedom and justice has to be first believed before it can be achieved.

It is another song about these guys hanging on to the fraying thread of faith in spite of what is going on around them: "And if the darkness is to keep us apart/ And if the daylight feels a long way off/ And if your glass heart should crack/ And for a second you turn back/ Oh, no, be strong." Bono's perseverance that he yearns to transmit to Suu Kyi may have its basis in his love of Scripture. When the apostle Paul says nothing on this earth can separate us from the love of God (ROM. 8:38, 39), it is a promise they could see through the many dark nights of the soul.

But the cover and title have yet another, spiritual and heavenly dimension. When U2 sang "Walk On" at the telethon for the heroes of the tragic events in New York, Washington and Pennsylvania on September 11, 2001, Bono spoke over the newly included hallelujahs on the emotionally charged climax,

"I'll see you when I get home"—an obvious reference to eternal hope even in the midst of mourning. The evangelical Christian roots from which Bono, Larry and The Edge came have a core belief that heaven is only achievable by belief. A new millennium, Jubilee 2000 and the loss of INXS singer Michael Hutchence may have brought a few spiritual issues to the forefront of the band's thinking. It was time to take stock and ask some serious questions. What goes in the suitcase, and what has to be left behind? What are the important things in life? What are the transitory things? What can last the journey? What is of the moment? These spiritual questions are an ongoing theme of the Bible.

Ecclesiastes has a basic thesis of "everything under the sun is transitory and is meaningless" (ECCLES. 1:2). Only a connection with God brings any sense to the meanderings of humankind. Jesus encourages His followers to forget about the treasures of earth because they get stolen or rust or moths eat them up. Treasures in heaven are lasting. The apostle Paul tells the early believers to put their trust not in things that cannot be seen because they are temporary, but to trust in things that cannot be seen because they are eternal.

At the end of the song, Bono lists the things that can be left behind: "All that you fashion/ All that you make/ All that you build/ All that you break/ All that you measure/ All that you steal/ All this you can leave behind." They are man-made things, but he adds to the list all the wrong things or mistakes that the Gospel deals with. Jesus came and died and was raised to life to offer a new start, leaving the regretful things and guilt behind and heading on afresh. The song and the Gospel have the same conclusions: "Love is not the easy thing/ The only baggage you can bring…" Jesus, when asked what the most important commandment was, told the enquirer, "Love the Lord your God with all your heart and with all your soul and with all your mind and with all your strength. The second is this: Love your neighbor as yourself." Whether you're heading for justice on earth or a fuller realization of the Kingdom of God in the next life, everything else can be left behind.

The soulful, Motown-sounding "Stuck in a Moment," which may become a U2 classic, was written about the suicide of Michael Hutchence, an event that hit Bono hard. He claims that the song is an angry conversation between him and his dead friend."[6] Yet the title itself is another moment when the transcendent belief at the core of U2, and indeed this album, suggests that there is more to this whole charade than the material world or the clock that seems to hem us in like walls to our left and right. It is so easy to get stuck in the moment of our troubled and hassled and painful and angry lives. But there is the hope of escape. If we could lift ourselves out of the moment and see all our moments from a panorama above us, then this moment in which we are trapped would hold new perspective. Ecclesiastes deals with this concept as well. There is nothing new under the sun, and if there is nothing above the sun, then this is all "meaningless, utterly meaningless" (ECCLES. 1:2, 9). But if there is something above the sun, then a different perspective comes to bear. That faith perspective, a belief in an eternal God, gives hope and strength in the moment to keep on keeping on, and the conclusion of the song almost becomes a brother of "I Still Haven't Found What I'm Looking For": "And if the night runs over/ And if the day won't last/ And if your way should falter/ It's just a moment/ This time will pass."

"Elevation," which follows "Stuck in a Moment," is the song that would have sat most comfortably alongside the *Pop* material. From being stuck in that moment, it prays for elevation that would give a higher perspective: "Love lift me out of these blues/ Won't you tell me something true/ I believe in you." Becoming the title of the tour to follow, "Elevation," like many songs on the tour, would take on a spiritual gospel feel. The "you" clearly becomes God. Elevation is about revelation and in the power of the live show touches close to transfiguration, a mystical experience that Jesus shared with a few of his disciples on a mountainside.

"Kite" seems to be Bono the magpie at work again, picking up scraps of thoughts and ideas and weaving them into another song of a hundred angles. From flying kites on Killiney Hill with his daughters, Eve and Jordan, to thinking about all that this world might throw at you like an unseen wind, this is a meditation on dying and pondering on whether we live life to its fullest. During a gig in Manchester, England, in August 2001, Bono dedicated the song to his father, who was dying of cancer and had just a few days to live. "I wrote this for my kids, but now I feel like he wrote it for me."

There is an overriding thought from John 3:8, where Jesus tells Nicodemus that the wind blows wherever it pleases; no one sees where it comes from or where it is going. Jesus was referring to the believer in that conversation, but that's the root of Bono's idea. Like a kite blowing about in the spirit unseen. This might be a moment when he is meditating on who his children will become in this unpredictable world and asking himself what they think of their father up until recently dressing up in make-up and horns in front of thousands of people every night.

"In a Little While" is about journeying home, and in this home, the singer will no longer be "blown by every breeze." There is autobiographical information in it. Bono seems to look back at his love with Ali and that line that harks back to the early days of U2 when it lived this tension between Lypton Village, the world of rock music and the Shalom fellowship: "Friday night running to Sunday on my knees." On the Elevation tour, after the death of punk rocker Joey Ramone, the song took a new turn. Apparently, Ramone was listening to this song at the end of his battle with cancer. Bono prefaced the song by telling the crowd: "He turned this song about a hangover into a gospel song. That's how cool Joey Ramone is."

"When I Look at the World" is one man's desire to have a mind like Jesus. It is full of U2 honesty in that it speaks with Jesus about the difficulties of acting like Jesus in every situation. The song starts out as an affirmation of how Jesus changes the singer's life, then it addresses the struggle: "So I try to be like you/ Try to feel it like you do/ But without you it's no use/ I can't see what you see/ When I look at the world." It is about trying—and struggling—to see the events of "Peace on Earth" from the other side of his dialogue with God.

"Grace" is an epic end to *All That You Can't Leave Behind.* It is an atmospheric ballad in the tradition of "One" or "With or Without You," but is more like "40" or "MLK." The ethereal mood is topped with the most beautiful poetry that evokes the grace of that word's other definition: "Grace/ She carries a world on her hips/ No champagne flute for her lips/ No twirls or skips between her fingertips/ She carries a pearl in perfect condition."

In a world where the eastern religions get a great deal more acceptance on the scale of cool than Christianity usually receives, Bono pulls a subtle little punch for the Christian belief in salvation by singing: "She travels outside of karma/ She travels outside of karma." There is something about grace that makes even those who believe in it find it hard to believe in. You can hear the words and take hold of the understanding that here is an upside down world order where the first are last and the last are first and where acceptance is unmerited. In a world where the first are first, and the only way to be affirmed is to be the most intelligent or best-looking or most successful, it is hard to get reconditioned to the conditioning of grace. A flower doesn't bloom in one hour of sunlight, and a believer's soul needs constant exposure to the rays of grace day after day, year after year, before it moves from an intellectual assent to a truth that our lives bask in and live by.

The fact that the members of U2 were all about to hit forty in the year of their ninth album's release must also have led to some soul-searching. You can drift through your thirties without noticing that middle age is a whole lot closer than youth. That you are being adored by fifty thousand young rock fans every night, dressed up in all the latest fashions, and rocking and rolling can hold back such an awareness. But the band members' seeing themselves twenty years older than those at the top of the charts must have had its impact on where they should go next. Could they compete? Grace may have become a friend worth getting to know at this stage.

As they took to the stages of the world on the Elevation tour to promote *All That You Can't Leave Behind,* U2 was experiencing the unmerited favor of God. The band had not shown such a spiritual openness or intensity for many years. As it ended the show with "Walk On," Bono would shout, "Unto the Almighty, thank you! Unto the Almighty we thank you!" before leading the crowd in choruses of "Hallelujah!" When Rolling Stone caught up with Bono in Atlanta, he was open about what he thought was going on: "God is in the room, more than Elvis. It feels like there's a blessing on the band right now. People are saying they are feeling shivers—well, the band is as well. And I don't know what it is, but it feels like God walking through the room, and it feels like a blessing, and in the end, music is a kind of sacrament; it's not just about airplay or chart positions."[7]

SOURCES

1 Olaf Tyaransen, "U2: The Final Frontier," (Dublin) *Hot Press*, 8 November 2000.
2 Danny Eccleston, "The Elastic Bono Band," *Q*, November 2000.
3 Joe Jackson, "Waiting for Beckett," (Dublin) *Hot Press*, 14 February 2001.
4 Ibid.
5 Ibid.
6 Chris Heath, "U2: Band of the Year," *Rolling Stone*, 15 January 2001.
7 Chris Heath, "U2 Tour: From the Heart," *Rolling Stone*, 10 May 2001.

»

from
Walk On: The Spiritual Journey of U2

Steve Stockman is a Presbyterian minister in Ireland where he works in the Chaplaincy at Queen's University in Belfast. He is a regular speaker at conferences and festivals, and has his own radio show on BBC Radio Ulster.

GOD IS IN THE HOUSE

BY STEVE STOCKMAN

«

» The members of U2 have been focused and clinical in their ambition to be the biggest band in the world. They've arguably been at the pinnacle of their profession for most of the past two decades, but Bono has never confined the meaning of his life to mere pop chart statistics. The music is simply the place where this Irishman makes rhyme and reason out of the big questions of life. Who are we? Why are we here? What has gone wrong? How can we put it right? For Bono it is about trying to find how a faith in God in a beautiful but sad and messed up world can work. He's a theologian, a social analyzer and political activist all rolled into one. Belief and activism are the things that drive him, and though the band may be less vocal they are happy to allow the front man to express their opinions.

In his graduation day speech at Harvard in June 2001, Bono was challenging and inspirational about the potential to change the world. Back in 1981, he said in U2's song "Rejoice," "I can't change the world, but I can change the world in me." U2 has seen the world since then and has come to dream the ideal that yes, the world can be changed, and these graduates from one of the world's most famous universities were not going to get off with a defeatist attitude. Bono wound up his speech saying: "We've got to follow through on our ideals, or we betray something at the heart of who we are. Outside these gates, and even within them, the culture of idealism is under siege beset by materialism and narcissism and all the other 'isms' of indifference." In general, materialism and narcissism are the very bedrock of rock 'n' roll—but not for Bono. Earlier in the speech, he defined rock as rebellion but then clearly defined the kind of rebellion that he was pontificating: "If I'm honest, I'm rebelling against my own indifference. I am rebelling against the idea that the world is the way the world is, and there's no damned thing I can do about it. So I'm trying to do some damned thing."

His speech gives us the honest and vulnerable Bono, the man who is prepared to rant and rave and allow his idealistic zeal take him across the lines of correctness and be accused of overdosing on sincerity or being foul-mouthed or idealistically naive. He is a man who, in the depth of his being, believes he cannot sit back and do nothing. Indeed he can do no other than give it everything, no matter what the consequences. The vociferousness of that—whether seen in his art, his politics, his faith or his life—often has received criticism from Christians thinking him too worldly and from the rock music press and fans for being too holy.

The complexities and spontaneous breakneck impulsiveness of U2's front man have fired what U2 is. That they were scruffily bound in a spiritual passion has given the band's blaze a unique twist and tale. When the Spirit Who roams his soul meets the adrenaline pumping feverishly in his red-blooded Irish veins, the fuse is lit to create an explosive live spectacular. But more than that, the fuse is lit to make him the hugest of rock personalities, not in any Jim Morrison-type, hedonistic, destructive way, but in a way that prods and provokes the entire world with alternative ways of living. As he said to the graduates: "Isn't 'Love Thy Neighbor' in the global village so inconvenient? God writes us these lines…we have to sing them…take them to the top of the charts, but it's not what the radio is playing, is it? I know."

Maybe it has been that subversive spirit, energized by the words of Jesus, that has kept U2 returning to the creative and commercial heights again and again. Maybe God is more obviously in the house than in that decade of horns and shades. But he has been on the lines and between the lines of U2's entire catalog, whether throwing beams of illumination across the band's study of the dark terrain of the modern world or shining brightly on albums such as *October* and *All That You Can't Leave Behind*.

The God dimension to U2 may be the reason why these guys stand unique in the realm of their chosen, or thrust-upon-them-like-a-gift-from-above, vocation. What other band is still producing anything as fresh and original twenty years into its career? What other band is giving the live act the kind of constant reinvention or passionate performance that U2 is doing? What other band is still living in the same place, with the same school friends? What other band has been able to maintain its sense of privacy and has given the press so little opportunity for tabloid headlines? What other band has added to its art the desire to use its status to do more than make money and enjoy the fame? What other band has such a sense of vocation, a vocation that seeps through every pore of its recorded and live work?

As its Elevation tour rolls across America, Europe and the world, U2 is reaching out to a new generation of fans who are discovering the band's back catalog for the first time, sending albums such as *The Joshua Tree* back up album charts. And the members of U2 know now more than ever that nothing matters more than God's love and grace, which can change everything. It is intriguing that the openness of the band's faith has coincided with a return to the primary colors of rock that broke the band out of Dublin more than two decades ago. It is intriguing too that U2's return to some spiritual and political soapbox proclamation has been accepted whole-heartedly by the rock audience of the third millennium. The Church could almost pack up its contemporary music stall that it has resourced for forty years and head back home because on the Elevation tour, U2 has done what that industry has aimed to do—involve Jesus in the conversation of a generation. As the band's concerts finish with communal choruses of hallelujah just as they used to finish with Psalm 40, concert halls are taking on the spiritual feel and emotion of cathedrals and churches. God is in the house, and the world is there to meet with Him.

»

From
Walk On: The Spiritual Journey of U2

Steve Stockman is a Presbyterian minister in Ireland where he works in the Chaplaincy at Queen's University in Belfast. He is a regular speaker at conferences and festivals, and has his own radio show on BBC Radio Ulster.

Wrestling with God

By Rick Diamond

The Jesus that I encounter in the gospels is not tidy. He isn't safe. He isn't a three-point sermon; He's more like an unpredictable series of explosions going off. He's a threat to almost everything—except those who are broken, lost, and open. Those whose houses have been picked up by tornados and flung across the sky. Those who have ended up in the desert. Jesus went to the desert. He knows what it is. He has His sacred wounds.

Because of this, Jesus is completely free. He isn't interested in anyone's rules or ideas. He is immoral in the very best sense of the word; the morals and conventional wisdom of the culture are his enemies. Jesus' job is to set people free, as He says in His first sermon in his home church, quoting a poem written a few hundred years earlier by an Israelite prophet:

> The spirit of the Lord has come into me.
> It has chosen me to give the poor some good news.
> It has sent me to go tell prisoners that they are to be set free,
> And I am to make the blind see again,
> And I am to give oppressed people relief.
> I have been chosen to tell everyone that the time is here
> when all debts are cancelled and all sins forgiven.
> God approves of you. You are free.[1]

Radical stuff. Culture-shattering. If Jesus' plans come true, no institution that is based on rules and regulations can remain standing. And the strange thing is that this statement by Jesus about His central purpose is supposedly one of the foundations of Christian theology and practice, but most churches in the West accomplish the exact opposite of this mission statement of Jesus'. But Jesus is undeterred.

For Jesus, to be modern is a sin—in the sense that Jesus repeatedly reacts against there being one answer. Jesus went to church and studied the Scriptures like a good boy, but He also threw furniture around in the church when He saw that what the Church really wanted was not to be an instrument of God's heart, but to maintain its hold on its own power. I mean, He literally threw furniture and beat people in the church office and the capitol building with a whip.

Jesus broke every rule and moral code He could find. He broke rules about how you had to prepare for meals, where to sit at a formal dinner, how to speak respectfully to those who were supposed to be honored, and how to respond to political power. He loved whores and their pimps; the dope-dealers and the bikers; the jocks and the stoners; the ex-cons and the manual laborers. He was one of them, one of the poorest of the poor, an outsider from birth. He loved to drink and laugh and dance. He also would weep wildly when His heart was broken. He believed that there are some things worth standing up for. He also believed passionately that there are some things worth standing up against, which for Him was anything having to do with religion's monopoly on truth, and its refusal to include people who didn't possess the right answer or act the right way.

The caretakers of the institutions demanded that the rules Jesus broke were non-negotiable. He'd respond that God was fed up with them and that God was going to throw them out like trash into a burning garbage heap outside of town, which was named Gehenna, which is translated, hell. Go to hell, religious people, Jesus said.

Jesus refused to be categorized. Every denomination and political party wanted Him to join their cause, and He refused. He knew that God is bigger than any man-made thing, any one way of seeing. He did not behave. He committed every kind of blasphemy. And yet, He believed that the ultimate blasphemy was to say you know the right answer—which in the first century was the equivalent of the modern mind of the twentieth century.

Jesus said repeatedly that there is no one right answer. There are many answers. "I have flocks you don't know anything about," He told His followers. Basically, "You're not the center of the universe. Get over yourselves." The leaders of the institutional church would tell Him that He was wrong to welcome and embrace people who hadn't been to Bible study, or said the correct creeds, or whatever. Jesus would tell the leaders to shut up and leave God's people alone. The leaders within His own movement came to Him at one point and complained, "There are other churches out there that are using your name to heal people! Give us the okay to make them stop!" What they were saying was, "That's not right! It's not fair! They don't belong to our club! They can't possibly be right! We're the only ones who are right!" Jesus' response to them was: "Leave them alone. They're not against us, so they're for us." That is, "You're not the only ones with a connection to God. Leave other people alone. Lots of others besides you will be doing what my Father wants for the people of the world."

Jesus included everybody. He healed everybody. He forgave everybody. He accepted everybody. He threw grace and wholeness around randomly, like a farmer sewing seeds in a field, hoping they'll take root. The leaders of the big denominations would insist that He stop celebrating so much. Jesus would tell them that God's love transforms everything into one big banquet —and that they wouldn't be allowed inside if they didn't stop being so self-righteous. They decided that they had to shut Him up somehow, which would eventually mean that He'd have to be executed. He expected that. So He promised them: "God's love is so powerful, you can shut me up for a day or two, but I can't be contained. I am a sign of God's grace. God is wild. You can't keep me in a box or a tomb or a religion or whatever. God's love will break the door down." That's what Jesus' resurrection is about: God's love breaking out of the box. It's too bad religion keeps trying to put Him back in.

One of the images of the Spirit of God used in the middle ages in northern Europe is the wild goose—it flies around wherever it wants to and lands where it will. You don't hold onto safe answers when you know the Spirit; you give them away and just fly. You don't know where you're going next; Jesus just says, "Follow me." In order to follow something that wild and free, someone that liberating and empowering, you're going to have to let some things go. Just as was true with entering the desert, it becomes time to let go of our weapons and just walk in. But following the Spirit doesn't lead you to become something less than you are; you become something more. You are free to grow larger and larger, stronger and more courageous, because you're free to let everything go.

Jesus' temptations were about letting go of the desires He had to be powerful and important. He let those desires drop by the side of the road He was walking, and then traveled easier and faster. That's why Jesus gave to His followers this gift: "Anyone who wants to be one of my followers should pick up a cross and follow me"—pick up an instrument of execution, and when you face the death of whatever needs to go, you'll be ready to see the presence of God in your everyday life. You think that if you start letting go, the thing that is going to die is you. But it's not. It's just stuff.

This is how Jesus can show love for His own executioners. The stories say that as He was dying on His cross, He prayed that God would forgive them—as Jesus was already forgiving them. He had let go of everything. And so His work was, as He said on the cross, finished.

If you are able to let go of everything that isn't necessary because you really don't need anything, then suddenly, as Richard Rohr says, everything belongs. All things become sacred because you accept that everything you experience is part of your journey. You don't have to hold onto anything or reject anything. All of your hates and loves, grudges and fears, joyous moments and celebrations—they're all sacred. All your wounds are sacred. All people are sacred, just as they are, already. You don't have to like everybody, but that's not the point. And so you're free to see it, decide if you want to carry it any longer, and keep traveling.

In one sense, Jesus' final assessment of His ministry—"It is finished!"—means, "It is alright. It is good. It is very good." How can someone who is facing death feel this? Because, as God says of the new creation He's spoken into being in the book of Genesis, whatever God does "is very good." This seems so contradictory to what Christians are taught. Yet it's so clearly what Jesus was all about—and it's the only God that the "we'll see" mind is ultimately really interested in. It's the God who is big enough to welcome every question and every experience.

The American poet Walt Whitman said, "Do I contradict myself? Very well then, I contradict myself. I am vast. I contain multitudes." Surely God is vast enough to contain multitudes of things that seem to us to be incompatible, but make perfectly good sense to God. "Oh, by the way, disciples—the laws of physics? We're going to throw those out today. Today we're walking on water." *That's impossible!* "Oh? Sorry—I just did it." Jesus refuses to see Himself as an answer-giver. One scholar says that Jesus is asked 183 questions in the gospels, and answers three. How not modern of Him.

God isn't an answer-giver either—read the Old Testament. God is stubbornly contradictory and complex. God is mystery. The night of His arrest, just before the soldiers are coming to arrest, torture, and execute Him, Jesus begs his Father to come up with another plan. What He hears from God is silence. And Jesus understands. So, accepting this deep within, He says, "Alright. This is what you and I have decided together to do. It's not the answer I want, but it's what has to happen." It's no surprise; this willingness to live without external surety is Jesus' consistent way of living and teaching. He lets go—and gets everything he ever wanted.

Freedom is terrifying. No one really wants to go to the desert and be stripped. No one wants to be that naked. No one wants to let go of everything. So we construct philosophies, answers, and doctrines that give us security and clarity. It can be very genuine to want a 1a God—one answer for all things.

But ultimately the "we'll see" mind can't be satisfied with one answer. Our experience is just too complex and rich. We embrace it, all of what it is, all of who we are. Then we are able to let go. And so we are free. Alanis Morissette sings in her song "Thank U," *The moment I let go of it/Was the moment I got more than I could handle/The moment I jumped off of it/Was the moment I touched down.*[2]

Jesus says that all we need is faith the size of a mustard seed, the size of a fat grain of pepper, the size of a grain of sand. Set down all those trunk loads of answers, and just walk. This makes sense to the "we'll see" mind. In the twenty-first century mind, all are welcome. For the children born during and after the 1970s, there aren't really any significant reasons to categorize people according to race, gender, sexuality, history, age, philosophy, denomination, or politics. I see people just hanging out together all the time. Postmoderns seek out people who are different from them. So the welcoming Jesus is a twenty-first century God worth knowing.

IF YOU AREN'T THERE

Spirit-space, the way of life that is about not knowing, is where there is room for something to happen that's more than achieving my to-do list. I'm not saying that you need to go to church so you can find something worth living for; I'd personally rather spend a day walking in the hills behind my neighborhood than spend a few hours at most churches. But that's my point. Walking in the hills, or listening to my son tell me about his latest school project, or talking to a good friend, or being silent and still, are all activities that we think of as sort of useless, and yet which create space. That space doesn't exist if the television is on or I'm frustrated about someone getting in front of me in traffic.

Poet Angelus Silesius writes, *God, whose love and joy are present everywhere/Can't come and visit you unless you aren't there.* This is difficult. Of course I'll be here; where else would I be? But the issue is, all the stuff that you hold onto is what keeps God from visiting—because you're not even where you are anyway. Your brain and soul are far from your body. You've pushed them away.

Spirit-space is about not knowing, getting out of the way. It's about silence. It's about surrender. When I was an English teacher, I used to reassure students that we weren't going to dissect the poems we were looking at; we'd try to let them live. To dissect something is to kill it. But of course, there was always a part of some of us, me included, which wanted to know the answer that would be on the test. So it's a struggle. I want to enjoy the spirit of Christmas, but I've also got to put up the stupid Christmas lights, so just hold on, Jesus, I'll get to you shortly. Thanks for stopping by, though.

Poet Natalie Goldberg says that when you're writing your own poem or story, if something that occurs to you seems particularly grisly or unpleasant, you should write about that. "Go for the jugular," she says. That's where the truth is.

Robert Bly, a writer who grew up on a Minnesota farm, had an alcoholic father and a strict church upbringing. He says that it was twenty years after he left home before he could even begin to have an honest thought or feeling. He began to come back to life by returning to Minnesota and sitting for hours in silence, waiting for an honest thought to come. Some of them did, finally, and his truest poems were born.

Your life is a story, a poem, or a song. It's a journey. Not to tell the truth means you miss it. Maybe you build something that has lovely craft and structure, but if it's not about the soul—which is contradictory, messy, terrible, beautiful—then it's not alive. It's not the truth. Or, as the Christian tradition says, it's not the Gospel.

At The Bridge in Portland, grace is messy. The community there is not tidy. To an outsider, the lack of structure doesn't seem to make sense. And yet it works. Kim, one of the women who leads Bible studies for the young adults, told me that what has helped her healing process is that the pastor, Ken, has "modeled his vulnerability for me." Ken is broken, too, just like everybody else there. That's the truth. And that's where healing comes from.

In the life that God is part of, what Jesus calls the Kingdom of God, everyone is in the doctor's office, everyone is sick, everyone is being healed. And so everyone belongs. That's why Jesus can invite everyone to the cross. That's where you get healed from being naked, wounded, bloody, and dying to becoming a new thing. That doesn't happen when you're standing solidly on the ground; it happens when you're hanging in the air, in between things. That's spirit space.

Entering that space is the truest purpose of prayer. Prayers can be formulaic; prayers can be spontaneous. Either way is okay. But I'm not talking about prayers—I'm talking about prayer, the means by which, when we are willing to enter spirit space, we hear what the Spirit is doing, breathing, singing, saying, being. Something we mumble in church or before we eat isn't what I'm talking about. Something the preacher says before a session of Congress isn't it either. Prayer is not knowing—and just going into that place. It can be by the side of a river, or in the car, or in the middle of an embrace, or in a hospital. But let's face it: Nobody really wants that very often. That's why we keep the DVD player on.

Jacob is finally ready to enter spirit space when he's at the river and ready to stop running. But the thing that comes to wrestle with him comes from the dark, and that's why we don't want to be in prayer—because we're afraid of what's in the dark. And it's not the stuff that's out there that scares us; it's what's within us, in the Shadow, the hidden thing we were told not to acknowledge or allow. However, the soul wants to talk to the Shadow. The soul wants to be in prayer. That's where God is, waiting to talk to us, when we get out of the way. Brent, a friend of mine who is facing a terminal illness, says, "The purification process is the beginning of mysticism. It's how we begin to see God." The purification he's talking about is the letting go and surrendering that ushers us into spirit space.

At his baptism, Jesus hears the voice of God affirm Him. Yet, on the night He is arrested, when Jesus asks God to come up with another plan than His crucifixion and death and what He hears is silence, out of that silence, Jesus accepts in the deepest part of Himself that His death is the ultimate reconciling, healing act He can make, and embraces it. That's spirit space.

A few years ago I was talking with a friend from church whose marriage was a total wreck and who was really in a lot of pain. He was trying to figure out whether to continue to try to make his marriage work, or get out of it, or drive off somewhere for a while. Here's one of our emails:

I need you to clear something up for me. I'm struggling with what the hell I'm doing wrong for God to want me on this road.

God doesn't want you on this road. This was never God's idea. God didn't want your mother to be alcoholic, your wife to be an alcoholic and emotionally cold, or your job to be in trouble. All that stuff is just what happens to human beings.

Am I not getting something? I'm starting to believe that I'm not getting the whole picture and I don't know if that's God saying I need to wake up.

A] There is no whole picture that's a clear answer. B] God is always wanting us to wake up, but it's never because He's frustrated that we're not understanding something. God is patient. But the bad place where we don't know the answer is a place where we can get healed up if we'll be still and not try to fix it first.

Well then, am I just setting myself up for failure? Am I screwing up?

You are doing what God wants for you, for everybody, which is, to face the truth, and be real, and have courage, and find how to stand on your own even in the face of huge pain. It will suck. It will feel like failure. But everything ends up being frustrating in one way or another. So, the answer is … pray, pray, pray. Be honest about what you're feeling, but don't demand anything from God just because you're in pain. You don't want a quick answer to this; you want the real answer. The thing you are wanting isn't in whether your circumstances are going nicely. So ordering God to fix it for us is like a toddler yelling at the mom to hand over the toy the toddler is already holding. Peace is already here. It's already possible. But we have to learn to be still. And that's what sucks. You're in pain and you don't want to be still; you want to move. But the healing is in being exactly where you are.

Being where you really are means that you awaken, and you accept what is—which means that you're not running. Peter Gabriel's song "Only Us" contains these lines:

> It wasn't in the words that kept sticking in their throats
> It wasn't with the angels in their quilted coats
> These battered wings still kick up dust
> Seduced by the noise and the bright things that glisten
> I knew all the time I should shut up and listen
> And I'm finding my way home from the great escape
> ....
> The further on I go, oh the less I know
> Friend or foe, there's only us.[3]

Gabriel wrote the song during a difficult time in his life, when he and his wife were going through a divorce. You can feel it. It's a song about giving up, and stopping, and just being where you are, so you can begin to heal.

In that healing process, you find something worth living for. That's the tricky part.

Andy Crouch, who speaks about postmodern spiritual growth, said at a conference a couple of years ago that in every way except one, the postmodern generation is letting go of the trappings and values of their modern parents and grandparents, but the one thing nearly everyone in America, young or old, can't let go of is consumerism. We can't stop consuming, eating, buying, wearing, driving, having. It's fun. It's a way of making your entire life like watching soap operas or music videos all the time, night and day, laughing and feeling like you're as cool as they are. But ultimately, that's not the good news. It doesn't heal.

The real thing worth wrestling is larger than that. You find something that matters, something that takes you beyond your own comfort, and slowly or suddenly your life is actually worth living, deeply and profoundly. You breathe deeper, like someone out playing Ultimate Frisbee or dancing or slowing down. You're awake. And you're wrestling in the best sense. It's like feeling ready to start playing racquetball with someone who plays better than you do so that you'll have to work harder. You start playing your life with something bigger than you. You breathe hard. You're cycling up a huge hill. It hurts. Jesus is in pain in the garden before His arrest—"I am deeply troubled," He tells His friends. "So I want you to pray for me." They fall asleep. But He's very awake. He has grasped a purpose larger than His own needs. And it's very good. It's actually worth doing. Incubus sings a song called "Drive" about this process of becoming an active participant in the direction of your life without grasping or controlling:

> Sometimes, I feel the fear
> Of uncertainty, stinging clear.
> And I can't help but ask myself
> How much I'll let the fear
> Take the wheel and steer ...
> But lately I am beginning to find that I
> Should be the one behind the wheel ...
> Whatever tomorrow brings, I'll be there.[4]

Truly letting go, releasing what the Buddhists call "attachment," is not about laziness or uselessness. It's the opposite. One of my heroes is my friend David. He is a fifty-year-old single dad of three teenage daughters, two of whom are in high school, and the other is in college. His wife left him ten years ago, and though he worked hard to repair his marriage, she decided she didn't love him anymore and that was that.

Over the years, he's done amazing things to be there for his daughters—even though he's also one of the ministers at my church, and a youth minister on top of that, which means he's available for a few hundred teenagers all the time, leading summer camps, going to football games, putting on Friday night worship services, and on and on and on. Wherever his wife moved over the years, he'd send his daughters to visit her, even driving them a few hundred and then driving back, and then making the loop again at the end of the visit. He coaches their ball games. He buys their prom dresses. And he will sit and listen to one of the high school students at our church for hours.

David is one of the most spiritually mature and compassionate people I've ever known. I've asked him how he's managed to survive over the years, and he smiles and shrugs and says, "It's just what you do." He hasn't dated. He says, "Right now, my job is to be there for my girls." He looks tired sometimes, but is almost always joyful. David has figured something out. He is tied to something. He has loyalty to something worth living for. He's not bitter, although he carries his wounds and knows pain. But his wounds have become sacred wounds, and he is a healed person—not because he's perfect, but because he's in love with something worth living for. Ironically, he reminds me of my great-grandfather, who lived simply and provided for his family, and was content that that would be his life's meaning. The difference is, Granddaddy didn't know of any alternative. David's had any number of ways out, like all of us in the twenty-first century, but he keeps deciding to take up his cross, and let some things die, so that his heart will live. And it does. And because he is being healed, he is a mighty healer.

To embrace your struggle is to make it holy. To wrestle with God breaks us and heals us. It gives us a new name. It brings us back home—but not to the same mess we left. We're not that person anymore. To say, "Yes, this is where I am and who I am," is holy. It's where we are, and it's where God is as well. We meet God there. It surprises us—or not.

This is a mystery. It cannot be gotten or grasped. But it is available. It is not something you can buy or trade for or earn. It is also not something that will happen by itself. We will hear it; it will brush past us, if we are willing to allow some space for it, to get out of the way, to be still, to let darkness come. It turns out it's not darkness after all; the sun is coming up. We "step out in faith" as the saying goes, but not because when we arrive on the other side, we'll meet God. The other side isn't where God is.

This is the secret: God is in the step itself. I know the "we'll see" mind can accept this; I've seen it happen. Postmoderns are already hungry for this and prepared for it. But that doesn't make it easy. But it's still good. It's your journey. It belongs to you. Breathe it. Walk it.

SOURCES

1 Jesus, in Luke 4:17-19, quoting Isaiah 6.
2 Alanis Morissette, lyrics, "Thank U," *Supposed Former Infatuation Junkie*, c1998 Maverick Recording Company, 9-47094-2.
3 Peter Gabriel, "Only Us," *Us*, songs published by Real World Music Ltd, Hidden Pun Music Inc., c1992 The David Geffen Company, GEFD 24473.
4 Boyd, Einziger, Katunich, Kilmore, and Pasillas, "Drive," Incubus, *Make Yourself*, c1999 EMI April Music Inc./ Hunglikeyora Music., c1999 Sony Music Entertainment Inc., 63652.

»

from
Wrestling With God

Rick Diamond is Pastor of Discipleship at Riverbend Church in Austin, Texas, in addition to serving as an adjunct faculty member at Drew University in the Doctor of Ministry program.

» NOTES